MW00773684

Jennette Eveline Evans McKay

MOTHERS OF THE PROPHETS
SERIES

Jennette Eveline Evans McKay

By
Lisa J. Peck

CFI
Springville, Utah

ISBN: 1-55517-877-4
e. 1

Published by CFI,
an imprint of Cedar Fort, Inc.
925 N. Main, Springville, Utah, 84663
www.cedarfort.com

Distributed by:

Cover illustration by Dale Mortimer
Cover design by Nicole Williams
Cover design © 2005 by Lyle Mortimer

Printed in the United States of America
10 9 8 7 6 5 4 3 2 1
Printed on acid-free paper

Dedication

To Brooke, my happy sunshine and beam of light.
Also, a special thank-you to Tiffany M. Jones and Doug Harris
for their great research, Dennis L. Davis for his valuable information on Wales, and, of course, my great writer friends for their
critical eye and loving support.

Contents

Chapter 1

My Beginnings

Batter my heart, three-personed God; for you
As yet but knock, breathe, shine, and seek to mend;
That I may rise and stand, o'erthrow me, and bend
Your force to break, blow, burn, and make me new.
I, like an usurped town, to another due,
Labor to admit you, but O, to no end;
Reason, your viceroy in me, me should defend,
But is captived, and proves weak or untrue.
Yet dearly I love you, and would be loved fain,
But am betrothed unto your enemy.
Divorce me, untie or break that knot again;
Take me to you, imprison me, for I,
Except you enthrall me, never shall be free,
Nor ever chaste, except you ravish me.

—John Donne, Sonnet 14

My soul can hardly contain the jubilee I feel here in Huntsville, Utah. The wind chills my face as I watch the gathering storm, and I am absorbing the power, the artistry, the wildness of the dark clouds on the horizon. Witnessing nature in such full, unyielding display testifies to me of the magnificence and supremacy of God. I glory in his goodness, his greatness, the active part he plays in my life.

Anticipating the downpour, I cannot help but reflect on the storms of my own life. When I recall Heavenly Father's work within me, I am left breathless. His influence bore me across the great Atlantic Ocean, across the vast country, and across many hardships to allow me the privilege of finally seeing "the tint and radiance of his countenance."[1]

The wind tickles my flesh. Goose bumps chase around my arms. It's more than the cold that brings this reaction. It is the remembering. The chill, the dampness, the overcast sky, and the green of the landscape take me back to my early days in Wales. Aye, they were good, long days that taught me many lessons.

When I was a lass, I stood on the crest of a hill as I do this day, fixed upon the approaching rain. In those times, I thought I knew how my life would go. As a child, I closed my eyes and saw it all unfold before me. I would live a simple, God-fearing existence supporting the Prophet Joseph Smith, along with a husband who adored me. In our simple cottage that he built with his own hands, we would nestle amidst the gorgeous, rolling hills and ravines of the

Welsh landscape. With the best-behaved and most bonny children in tow, I would thrive with my husband. We would never have too many hardships, and all our children would miraculously survive any illness that swept through the village. Work would be available aplenty to my husband, who I hoped could escape the incessant dirt and misery that the coal mines created for my papa.

I wished fortune would grin upon us, enabling my husband to provide for the family while doing work he enjoyed and would help build up Zion at the same time. I would have the pride that only a wife whose husband lives righteously can possess. In my spare moments, I'd turn to the handiwork that would fetch a high price and bring in extra money so that our family might obtain a few luxuries like books and china. I would learn the organ and would play at church meetings, lifting spirits. My neighbors would all eventually become Saints. What I imagined was an earthly sojourn like my parents' life but better.

Many of the things I foresaw in my life came true. Some did not. Others, as I am sure is the way for all mortals, struck me with total surprise and could have only been God's doing. Let me tell you about the storms, the sunrises, and the sunsets of my life.

Wales

There is something about the small mining village in South Wales that still stirs my heart, calls to my roots, my people, my spirit. Think of a place with velvet green rolling over expansive, low mountains, lush deep valleys that contrast with the rich blue sky and creamy white clouds. Imagine the one place on earth where the sun saves its most majestic colors for the sunsets. In this place there is a home called Plasagon House, in the town Cofen Coed, near Merthyr Tydfil. I came to earth on this spot on August 23, 1850.

My parents, Thomas and Margaret Powell Evans, owned a pleasant house among other row houses that meandered through our small village, which looked out onto the glorious countryside. Papa had been born in Glamorganshire, South Wales, in October 1812. He came from a long line of lawyers, ministers, and teachers.[2] We owned a comfortable sofa, a large table, and one of the most beautiful finely crafted mahogany chest of drawers that I have ever seen. The bedroom had "the six-foot bed cover[ing] the entire width, and its length [was] barely two feet longer than it [was] wide, and the old rafters . . . about eight feet high."[3] Before the trouble began, my family lived comfortably from the rent of several homes my parents owned.

The mining village, although striking in its scenery, became tainted from "the perpetual smoke and constant din of the forges."[4] This problem would only increase when the furnaces were opened in the darkness of the evening. At these times "the sky looked as if a blazing volcano were erupting."[5] The ferocity of the fire scared me when I was a lass of two, three, and four. I clung to the security of Papa's leg until he bent over to pick me up. Then my arms wrapped tightly around his neck, and I felt safe against his strong body. Oft times I wore smudges of dust all over my clothes from this embrace, because he would have recently arrived home from working in the coal mines. Mama fussed about the mess. 'Twas her constant battle to keep the children and our home clean.

Besides clinging to Papa's neck, I remember so well wandering up the nearby stream to find my stone. Now, my stone was a special one shaped like a chair. It fit perfectly, as though made for me. Many an enjoyable time I slipped my shoes off and sat on the rock with my feet dangling in the cold water. Other times I stood atop of what we called a mountain. There, in the midst of the trees, I felt the dampness from the ocean blow against my skin.

My thoughts wandered to the death of my three siblings—my two-year-old sister and the baby twins, a boy and girl. My siblings died from sickness when I was four years old. I often wondered what they did in heaven. They must be happy there, I thought, as I reflected on the fact that they were with Jesus and I would have to wait my turn. Sometimes I closed my eyes and tried to see them and figure out what they looked like, but I never had much luck.

I was blessed, Mama would tell me, because I knew where my siblings were and that they were safe. She said many people did not understand that God was a loving God and that he made everything all right in the end. She told me how she and Papa did not have a complete understanding of this until right before my birth when a knock on the door came . Mama found a scraggly missionary who wanted to share a message from God. He spoke of God's love and how the gospel was restored to the earth as in former times. God wanted each of us to be in his kingdom in the next life and for us to help build up Zion in this one. As she, Papa, and my older siblings listened to his words, Mama said she could not hold back the overwhelming desire to do all that our Maker required of her so that she could remain with her family after death. The rest of my family must have felt the same because they were all baptized into the Church in May 1850, except those who were too young. When the age was right, the others would follow the light as well.

In that same year, the missionaries had found much success when one of the horrifying fires in the mine burst forth. The flames licked toward the workers, causing blistering on their skin. The smell of burning flesh filled the mines as the scorched victims were carried to the nearby stream. The wounded were doused with the dirty water and left to die. The women wept with joy when the missionaries showed up and healed the workers through the priesthood. These miracles brought many into the Church.

My parents' happiness with finding the gospel was soon lessened when word spread in the community about their new faith. My papa's family was among some of the town members who grew hostile over our conversion. My grandparents, Edward and Jennette Powell Evans, disowned my family and refused to see any of us again. This was difficult for us, having been close to Grandma and Grandpa Evans. Papa had thought for sure his papa would accept the word but soon realized he wouldn't. My grandfather's rejection of Papa and our family, and also the gospel, deeply saddened Papa. His shoulders often sagged under the burden. But that was not the only trouble our family faced for accepting the truth in our lives. Joining the Church set off the persecution commonly directed at all of its members. This hatred was especially aimed at Papa because he was ordained an elder by William Richards. Later he became the president of the Merthyr Tydfil Conference of the Church, or in other words, the branch in the area. I will not go into the details of what occurred in Wales, trying to keep a spirit of forgiveness about me. Reflecting on our troubles stirs up resentment. Our situation became grave enough that our family decided to gather with the other Saints in America to build up Zion. Truth be told, I think Papa was anxious to find a new life where there was more possibility of making a difference. I believe he wanted to be with like-minded people. I grew up on the stories of how he "sold his possessions for a fraction of their worth."[6]

Before we left, Mama gave birth to my wee sister, Lizzie, on March 27, 1856. She turned out to be the youngest sister. I loved holding her, singing whatever Celtic song floated into my mind. She was a bonny girl, with a smattering of hair and large eyes that Mama predicted would turn brown and intense like mine.

I thought we were being tested enough by having to leave our beautiful homeland, our friends, and to flee from our enemies, but the Lord must have wanted to give us an Abrahamic test of faith. A terrible event happened soon after Lizzie's birth. My oldest brother, about to celebrate his eighteenth birthday on May 28, passed away days before we left for America.

At the time, I was six and could not accept that he had gone. I often asked for him, which I imagine this constant longing for my older brother reopened the wounds of my parents. Later in life, I have talked to Mama about this. She informed me that Edward's passing struck her extra hard, especially with the realization that soon the family would depart for Deseret. She told me in later years, "I condemned the Lord in my heart for having taken our main help on the journey ahead of us, and I said in my heart, 'Lord, if you had to take any of my children, why didn't you take this little helpless baby and leave us the oldest son to help us on the journey across the ocean and across the plains?'"[7]

When Mama spoke, I sensed her deep pain over losing a precious son. She pressed her lips firmly together, which she often did when she resolved to move forward. Finally she said, "I was wrong in my judgment. God knew best, and I should have trusted him. You see today how blessed I am, living here with the comfort I have of Lizzie, my youngest child, now the mama of three boys, and my comfort in my old age. God looked farther into the future than I could."[8]

Although I was young, I remember the graying color in my parents' faces and the tears brimming in Mama's eyes when she paid one last visit to the graves of her five children. There was Morgan, who died at birth in 1846. He came before I arrived. After my birth, my sister Margaret died at the age of two. That year was a hard one full of loss for our family. We not only lost Margaret but also twins at their birth—a girl and boy.

We were not the only family who lost loved ones. It was a

common occurrence. I heard it whispered that death took about a quarter of the young, but my family lost nearly half. Many infants succumbed to the attacks of various illnesses that infected the area, from black lung disease the miners become afflicted with, to scarlet fever, typhoid, measles, cholera, and whooping cough. There were six of us remaining: my sister Ann, sixteen at the time; Thomas, fourteen; Evan, twelve; Howell, ten ; myself, six; and Elizabeth, who we called Lizzie, an infant.

What must have been on my mama's mind as the wagon pulled away from her home and the resting place of her children? Did she recall her experiences giving birth to her eleven children? Did she reflect on the close friends she tearfully bid farewell and would never see again? Did she think about her family and the separation from them? Did she ponder the unkindness of her family and neighbors that must have made the decision to leave easier? Did she look at the small chapel where she married Papa on March 27, 1837? Would she miss looking back on the old building to remember the joy and hope of that occasion ? Did she reflect on the countryside where Papa proposed to her in the Welsh tradition by presenting her with a wooden spoon as a token of his love? What must Mama have been thinking as she gave up much of what was dear to her in order to pursue a chance at a better life by joining with the Saints?

As for me, six years of age, I was not afflicted with reflection. Instead I pestered my parents with a multitude of questions, anxious to engage in the adventure that awaited us.

I cannot think of a womanly virtue that my mama did not possess. Undoubtedly, many a youth, in affectionate appreciation of his mama's love and unselfish devotion can pay his mama the same tribute; but I say this in the maturity of manhood when calm judgment should weigh facts dispassionately. To her children, and all others who knew her well, she was beautiful and dignified. Though high-spirited she was even-tempered and self-possessed. Her dark brown eyes immediately expressed any rising emotion which, however, she always held under perfect control.[9]

—David O. McKay

Chapter 2

TRAVELING TO ZION

The greatest delight which the fields and woods minister is the suggestion of an occult relation between man and the vegetable. I am not alone and unacknowledged. They nod to me, and I to them. The waving of the boughs in the storm is new to me and old. It takes me by surprise, and yet is not unknown. Its effect is like that of a higher thought or a better emotion coming over me, when I deemed I was thinking justly or doing right.

—*Nature,* Ralph Waldo Emerson

When we departed for America, my heart, and I am sure others in the family felt the same, ripped from my chest. There was something about this land called Wales that had sunk deep within and become an important part of me. For the rest of my life, I heard its call.

As our wagon bounced along the rising hills, I wondered what lay before me. I wondered if I would ever see my homeland again.

Would I come back and marry a man here? Would Deseret be as green and breathtaking as this land? I heard from the missionaries that Zion was far away from the roar of the ocean. It had a great lake so full of salt that a person could float. Would that be as good as an ocean?

Our family soon made their way to Liverpool, England, where Papa planned on booking passage on a ship. We did so on the *Horizon,* May 22, 1856. Many people were packed aboard, six hundred of them Saints as ourselves, with the same burning igniting in their hearts to worship God. We gathered together in one heart to flee to Zion, that is in America to be with the pure in heart. We embarked on a great work to create "The Kingdom of God which . . . is not of this world, but the Kingdom of the Great God."[1]

Aye, while on the ocean, the boat rocked something awful as we crossed. Mighty waves rolled up and down as if we were rapidly ascending a mountain only to tumble down again. Many passengers including myself were sick.

Fortunately there were times when the water calmed and my stomach settled to a slight nervousness, and when I could slip away from Mama's grip and stand on the deck to feel the ocean spray sprinkle my face. This would remind me of standing in the midst of the trees on top of one of the mountains in Wales. In each place, so different from each other, I would ponder life as I stood in the mist.

During the trip there was one particular lady who stood on the deck alone, keeping her eye on a shark that followed us. She became increasingly despondent as she watched that shark. Her fearful cries caused many on the ship, including myself, to become alarmed. I was six and thus subject to wild imaginations. So I and many other superstitious sailors and passengers conjured up horrid scenes of being eaten by a menacing shark.

Mama sought to teach me that I could call on my Heavenly Father in circumstances like these, and that if I did so I would be protected. I spent much time praying in hopes of not being eaten. Other times my siblings, and other friendly children on the boat, distracted me in their games, and that kept my focus off possible doom. During this time I forged a good friendship with an English girl, Elizabeth.

I would say things like, "You know that the crew will sail this ship through any storm to meet their schedule. Our boat is going to sink. We are going to drown."

She laughed. "Our leaders made sure we only took the more sturdy boats."

"How do you know that?" I asked.

"My papa told me."

"Then we are going to die from measles or chicken pox," I said, crossing my arms over my chest. There was no way that the Church leaders could stop that. And we both knew of some passengers that were afflicted. "We're stuffed in this ship like packed rats. You know once one person gets a disease it spreads."

"You are silly," she said, and then distracted me with a game. "Stop being so afraid." These words came back to me throughout my years.

When the crew hatched us down in the bottom of the boat because of the storm, Elizabeth found me huddled in a ball crying. "Want to play a game?" she asked.

"We cannot," I said. "We can hardly see anything." Elizabeth knew that I was referring to the few lamps that hung in the corners, shedding only the faintest of yellow light.

"No, silly," Elizabeth said, jabbing me in the side. "We can make up stories. That's one of the best games."

Her ability to spin a tale was mesmerizing and would keep my attention until it was time to eat beef or pork, beans, and potatoes. Once we collected our food, one of the many children gathered around to hear about the princess's mighty adventures in the forest, would beg Elizabeth to continue with the adventure. The story telling passed the time when we were not attending religious services, prayer meetings, instruction classes, or reading.

Iowa and the Wagon

Once we arrived in America on June 30, we thought our travels would become somewhat easier. We were mistaken. Because our trip from England launched late, it put our handcart company under pressure to beat the pending snowstorms that come later in the year. We boarded a train to Iowa City with the other Saints from the Boston seaport. I remember with great fondness how much I enjoyed my first train ride. The wheels circling and dirty smoke snaking up into the air enthralled me. The noise thundered, and my little sister Lizzie cried. But, for the most part, I giggled.

Mama said that during the majority of the trip the children slept from the exhaustion of sailing across the rough Atlantic. The train experience ended July 8, 1856, and we faced yet more difficulties. The saints in Iowa City had not expected so many travelers. They lacked the supplies to accommodate everyone. Papa listened to Brother Brigham's counsel for the Saints to hold up and wait before crossing the plains. Wanting to make the travel as easy as he could on his family and wishing to lose no more members of our family, he and my mother decided to wait in Iowa until they earned money for supplies.

Papa spent much of his time listening to tales of crossing the plains. He heard of the many deaths, starvation, and loss of limbs that the earlier Saints experienced as well as stories of the horror experienced by pioneers when wagons tipped over during steep mountain climbs. Papa gained a better appreciation of why Brother Brigham advised the use of handcarts. Not only did the handcart seem an easier way to travel; it was also less expensive. Brigham Young wrote in the *Millennial Star:*

We cannot afford to purchase wagons and teams as in times past. I am consequently thrown back upon my old plan—to make hand-carts, and let the emigration foot it, and draw upon them [the carts] the necessary supplies, having a cow or two for every ten. They can come just as quick, if not quicker, and much cheaper—can start earlier and escape the prevailing sickness which annually lays so many of our brethren in the dust. A great majority of them walk now, even with the teams which are provided, and have a great deal more care and perplexity than they would have if they came without them.[2]

Papa worried that this type of travel would be too much for Mama, but she bravely reassured him the Lord would see her family through. We were on the Lord's mission, and He would provide a way for us to accomplish the task that lay before us.

Nevertheless Papa decided to travel by wagon. He wanted the protection the canvas could provide. He was also determined to leave in the early spring as an added measure to guard against the forewarned diseases. It took my family three years to get everything together in order for us to leave. The new language, different land, and new customs were all very overwhelming at first. Mama talked constantly about how much better it would be when we reached Zion, and we believed her. When at last our family had the provisions and equipment we needed, we set off with "a good team of horses to pull the wagon, a cow tied behind to furnish milk."[3]

My family set off from Florence, Iowa in the private company of Captain Philip H. Buzzard, whose name did not inspire confidence. We sought a place to live and work a long with the honest in heart. We left in the early spring of 1859. We traveled, mostly walking through the heat, dust, blisters, aches, and fatigue. The physical excursion proved exhausting. I thought we were struggling and hungry, but little did I know. The Saints who had traveled on the ship with us, around six hundred of them, would not wait to go to Deseret, and had left us behind. We heard reports back that 145 of those people died on that trek, including my dear friend, Elizabeth, from the ship. This news haunted me for years.

During the days on our trip when I was overcome with heat, I would remind myself of our friends and days like October 14, 1856, when the skies opened up, sending snowflakes down on the travelers. The temperature had dropped, and bitter cold seeped into their bones and joints, making their very souls turn into brittle icebergs.

To add to their misery, news came that the much longed for rescue wagons would not reach them for yet another eight to ten days. That meant they had to go another hundred miles before they received food. Supplies had shrunk down to mere scraps of food and the starvation was so severe it drove some to boil their shoes and eat them. Others could not keep themselves from gnawing the flesh on the joints of their fingers.

Dreams of food plagued me at night as I slept on the cold, rocky ground. As time passed, thoughts also came when I was awake. As I walked beside the wagon, straining to cross deep ravines, my mind pondered the next time I would be able to sink my teeth into a fresh biscuit or a sweet dessert or maybe an apple, orange, or peach.

When the hunger seemed too much, I focused my attention on a blade of grass or a shimmering leaf in a tree or some other beauty in nature, and then found my energy restored enough to go on.

I played with friends I had made. My eyes now have a tear as I think of their beautiful, happy faces and the games we used to share. We spent much time together laughing, and as we grew hungrier and tired, we talked about what our favorite meal was and what we would eat first if we had a feast laid out before us.

We also passed time by discussing the possibility of a transcontinental railroad across the country. The men often engaged in conversation about where the railroad should go. Sometimes we joined them in finding our favorite spots, other times arguing with whoever joined in the discussion as to why a particular location was not good.

We could feel God's active influence in our lives as he put his arm around us. I knew that our hardships were a small price to pay to show our alliance to him, the Almighty. It was a privilege to be involved in such a noble cause.

It took my family three years after leaving Wales before we rolled into Great Salt Lake Basin. When we did, it was worth all the misery and hardships we had gone through. Little did we know what miracles and trials laid before us.

Whatever was in store, I looked forward to being out of the

wagon, off the trail, and eating good vegetables like lettuce, carrots, broccoli, and fruits like apples, pears, and plums. I dreamed of taking a warm bath. I anticipated living in a cabin, which I prayed would be built quickly. Anxiousness filled me, as I wondered what we would encounter. I feared the Indians after hearing many a horror story from the boys on the trail. I hoped that rather than find these stories true, they would prove to be stories the boys told to scare. In my new home, I pictured picnics by the streams, dances at the churches, and many fashionable dresses for me to wear.

Her [Jennette Eveline Evans McKay] soul, to quote the words of the poet was, 'As pure as lines of green that streak the first white of the snowdrop's inner leaves.' In tenderness, watchful care, loving patience, loyalty to home and to right, she seemed to me in boyhood, and she seems to me now after these years, to have been supreme.[4]

—David O. McKay

Chapter 3

GATHERING SAINTS

Think not, when you gather to Zion,
Your troubles and trials are through—
That nothing but comfort and pleasure
Are waiting in Zion for you.
No, no; 'tis design'd as a furnace,
All substance, all textures to try—
To consume all the "wood, hay, and stubble,"
And the gold from the dross purify.
Think not, when you gather to Zion,
That all will be holy and pure—
That deception and falsehood are banish'd,
And confidence wholly secure.
No, no; for the Lord our Redeemer
Has said that the tares with the wheat
Must grow, till the great day of burning
Shall render the harvest complete.
Think not, when you gather to Zion,

The Saints here have nothing to do
But attend to your personal welfare,
And always be comforting you.
No; the Saints who are faithful are doing
What their hands find to do, with their might;
To accomplish the gath'ring of Israel,
They are toiling by day and by night.
Think not, when you gather to Zion,
The prize and the victory won—
Think not that the warfare is ended,
Or the work of salvation is done.
No, no; for the great Prince of Darkness
A tenfold exertion will make,
When he sees you approaching the fountain
When Truth you may freely partake.

—Eliza R. Snow,
"A Word to the Saints Who Are Gathering"[1]

The State of Zion

The Saints had an intense standoff against the United States two years before we arrived in Zion. This problem worried many of the migrating Saints, who wondered if once we were able to reach Zion, would it then be safe for us there. Would we be able to raise our family and practice our religion?

The problem escalated when the president of the United States,

James Buchanan, received faulty information that Deseret was rebelling against the United States. The president launched an army after the Saints called Johnston's Army.

The United States Army sent 2,500 men on the march to Utah. The battalion's orders were to replace Governor Brigham Young with the national appointee, Albert Cumming.

Our prophet was not going to take this threat lightly. We heard reports that Brigham Young told the saints to burn everything instead of surrendering to another mob that wanted to prevent us from worshiping God.

Brigham Young bravely declared, "There shall not be one building, nor one foot of lumber, not a stick, nor a tree, nor a particle of grass and hay, that will burn, left in reach of our enemies."[2]

The Saints fled to southern Utah until the storm passed. When Governor Cumming took office, he seemed fair and desiring to be of service to our people. There were many prayers of thanks offered when finally the Saints moved back to their homes.

Over the years, I have talked to many people who were there at that time. The women go into elaborate detail about the condition they found their homes in upon returning. The passing army took great liberties and left the Saint's residence's in a messy, depressed condition. As I trudged along the trails with my family, I wondered if something as threatening as Johnston's Army would be facing us once we reached our destination.

Coming to Zion

I will always remember August 24, 1859, with a special fondness and deep appreciation. On that blistering summer day, my family and I rode into the Great Salt Lake Valley. At last we had reached our destination, the Lord's promised land, where the Saints could live free from hatred and persecution. I hurried forward, through Parley's Canyon, looking at the city that Brigham and the Saints had built. Tears slipped from my eyes. We were here.

"Zion, at last," Papa called out with exuberance.

Mama nodded with a pleased smile. Soon after we rolled into town, Saints greeted us warmly. We stayed in the Great Salt Lake Valley for the next two weeks. During that time, my parents left us children to watch each other as they traveled around the surrounding area in search of a place to make our home. They could not stop talking about the land where "they decided to settle." It had trees, good soil, and was filled with wildlife and sweeping mountains —an area already lightly settled called Ogden. My parents "purchased property that is now between Adams and Madison Avenues and 28th and 30th Streets."[3] Ogden was a peaceful, small community filled with the songs of birds and scampering of other wild life, which let us know that God's grace resided there. It did not take long for my family to raise a temporary log cabin with the help of our neighbors. After we had provided ourselves with shelter, my parents meticulously planned our future home. Papa, accustomed to living comfortably, insisted on building the place right. After some years our permanent home, a four-room rock house, was one of the nicest homes in the area.[4] Everything was well thought-out and well built. We never needed to rebuild anything. Many admiring men came around to ask advise for their own places.

Deseret was anxiously engaged in many events during this time, including its involvement at the height of immigration. This required the resourceful and strong leadership of our prophet, President Brigham Young. His firmness, tempered with diplomacy in the struggles with the United States, often made up our dinner conversations.

Growing up in Ogden meant being swept away in the zeal of our faith. We set out to build a "holy nation," a "Zion" where God's elect would "be gathered in unto one place upon the face of this land!" (D&C 29:8). Daunting. The Saints strove together to realize the ideas of a Zion community like the one talked of in 3 Nephi after the Savior visited the American continent. We followed Brother Brigham's counsel to build up the principles of the united order, which on a practical level, meant becoming a self-sufficient people who labored together with a community spirit of brotherhood and sisterhood.

Of course not everyone embraced this great adventure, or the land for that matter. Mama told me of several women who complained about this area being "lifeless and tasteless." These women continued by saying they could "anticipate no rest or pleasure."[5] I noticed they were some of the unhappiest people in the community.

Despite some others' disappointment, my family enthusiastically dove into the work of settlement. We had not traveled a third of the way around the world to fail at our endeavor. Papa farmed and participated in many community projects, such as clearing the land for newcomers, constructing public buildings, and digging ditches and canals.[6] Mama not only gardened, cooked, sewed, and looked after we children, but also engaged in home spinning and dipping candles to sell. We strove to establish a community that "would never have to buy anything . . . and always have something to sell and bring money to help increase their comfort and independence."[7]

For my part, I "helped to gather fruits and vegetables to be bottled or dried and stored; learned how to make soap, butter, and tallow candles; and tended [my] little sister."[8] I also spent time with many friends and participated in gatherings with other girls to learn how "to make a quilt or rug, knit stockings, or peel peaches for drying. Dances were held nearly every Friday and special holiday,"[9] and I enjoyed being there with my friends and meeting the boys of the community. We, the youth in the town, also saw each other at church meetings, which included "Sunday School, sacrament meeting, fast and testimony meeting (held on Thursdays), ward parties and picnics."[10]

With all the struggles it took to set up our farm and to have it produce enough for us to live on, Mama still saw to it that I attend school. She believed the sacrifice was worth the benefit of having me educated. She would say, "Knowledge will be a great asset in your life and in the life of my future grandchildren."

I loved having this opportunity. My teachers taught the Second Ward School in Ogden with great enthusiasm and had skill in giving us our lessons. I learned from the best teachers in all of Zion: Harriet Canfield Brown and Rose Canfield. These women traveled from New York State where they graduated from an eastern academy. The good Lord sought to bring them to the gospel, to not only bless their lives but also the students'. Sister Brown heard about the gospel when she lived in Council Bluffs, Iowa in 1854. She enthusiastically accepted it, claiming she had waited for the truth all her life. In 1856 she journeyed to Ogden before my family. She helped create the Second Ward School under Bishop Edward Bunker's direction. Feeling overwhelmed by the task before her, she wrote and enlisted her younger sister, Rose, to serve as an assistant.

Both these women loved literature, history, and many other topics. I often stayed after school to discuss different books and authors with them. Their encouragements led me, with the help of my parents, to begin a lending library for my friends and family.

Sometimes this brought great amusement, especially when a male shyly came around hinting for a book. "Ms. Evans," they'd say, "Do you have any material that would be good for my mama, sister, grandmother to read?"

"Yes, I do," I'd say, gesturing for them to enter the house. "I have the perfect book of poems. I am quite confident that your mama, sister, grandmother will be much taken from Sonnet 29, written by Shakespeare."

They would clear their throat. "Maybe they might be interested in something else."

I thumbed through my books. "How about Emerson's insightful words on nature and how he became more in tune with God and his soul?" That book would be taken by the boy. Another favorite was Eliza R. Snow's work, where she explored our existence.

When the men or boys were leaving, I would call after them, "It says in the Book of Commandments 'all things unto [God] are spiritual.'" They'd nod. I have no doubt that reading and learning more of God through the great poets and sermons of earlier times aid the reader in pursuit of the spiritual realm.

Her [Jennette Eveline Evans McKay] influence and beauty entwined themselves into the lives of her sons and daughters as effectively as a divine presence.[11]

Chapter 4

LIFE IN ZION

Shall I compare thee to a summer's day?
Thou art more lovely and more temperate.
Rough winds do shake the darling buds of May,
And summer's lease hath all too short a date.
Sometimes too hot the eye of heaven shines,
And often is his gold complexion dimmed;
And every fair from fair sometimes declines,
By chance or nature's changing course untrimmed.
But thy eternal summer shall not fade
Nor lose possession of that fair thou ow'st;
Nor shall Death brag thou wanderest in his shade,
When in eternal lines to time thou grow'st.
   So long as men can breathe or eyes can see,
   So long lives this, and this gives life to thee.

—William Shakespeare, Sonnet 18

By 1867 I was teaching grammar school. As I instructed my students, attended church activities, enjoyed parties and other events, I had the pleasure of meeting many fine young men. These suitors had stellar qualities, but only one stuck out to me, a handsome lad with locks of thick, wavy hair and intense, dark eyes, David Oman McKay. He had a well-trimmed "General Grant" beard. Strong from working on his farm and possessing a charming Scottish nature, I could not help thinking about him after he left from the social functions where we saw each other.

He had a way of making me laugh by his comments, and he caused me to blush. For example, he'd often commented [how] my long, straight hair that I parted and tied in a bun at the nape of my neck was beautiful.[1] Over and over again, he said, "I love your hair."

On a deeper note, as I watched how this good-looking man conducted himself, I could see that his heart followed God. He did not shy away from work or service. His passion for creating the holy nation filled his speech. He often visited me after I finished a day of teaching and wanted to discuss what I thought about the transcontinental railroad that was coming. Did I think it would be a good thing to be connected to the gentile world or would it only bring problems?

I was impressed how David would ask my opinion and once I gave it, he valued it. We would discuss how the railroad would mean that more immigrants could come to Zion more quickly and without the difficulties the earlier pioneers had gone through. Was that a good thing? The gentiles brought money and opportunity, but they would also bring ideas and practices from the outside world. How was this going to affect our lifestyle?

David and I would often discuss at length the problems Brigham Young was engaged in as he struggled with the United States over a number of issues. One of his biggest problems was to keep teachers with religious commitments in the schools. The government seemed determined to keep God out of everything.

Not only would David Oman McKay talk about politics but also brag about his heritage. He came from the clan McKay, which had a history that could be traced back to the fourteenth century. This clan's royal roots derived from the houses of McEth and Moray. At one time their country covered five-eighths of the county of Sutherland, Scotland.

David would puff out his chest, and with an air of self-importance say, "I have a lord for my ancestor."

I would laugh. In effort to tease him I'd say, "I do not believe you."

"It is true." His hand touched his chest. He leaned forward as though injured by my words. "How can you not believe me? Sir Donald MacKay was the chief of the clan. He was a mighty leader. Through his valor, he was able to rise up an army of 3,000 men to be of service in Bohemia, and after that the men journeyed to Denmark. My ancestor was made Lord Reay in 1628 because of this great deed."

"Great deed, indeed," I said, laughing. "Where is this mighty Lordship now? Where is the vast land that your clan owned?" When he became too boastful I liked to remind David that his history was not as glorious as he made out. "David," I'd say in my teacher voice, "You know your history as well as I. Are you trying to hide the fact that in 1642 Lord Reay sold Strathnaver to the Earl of Sutherland? He was forced to pay the loans from providing for and moving 12,000 men, which he signed up in service to aid the Protestant cause in the great Thirty Years' War."

David laughed. "Paying such debts is not that difficult."

I then explained to him the high price this debt cost his clan. "The estates needed to be sold to the Countess of Sutherland. Then, tragically, the northern MacKay's were forced out during the Sutherland Clearances to make room for the sheep."

"True indeed," David said with a twinkle in his eyes. "But then my grandpapa became the Earl of Caithness and had close association with him and all in the household at Thurso Castle."

"David, I can tell that glory must have ended, because you are standing here before me and your family lives not too far away."

He scratched his head. "This is what I get for taking up with a teacher of history."

It was then that David told me the striking story that drew many parallels to my own. We sat under a tree to rest in the shade. He painted the picture of wild scenery where he used to live, with schools, churches, castles, and history. He came from the town called Thurso. His cottage was hidden behind shrubs with red berries. He took a path to the house constructed of flagstone. "There were yellow corn fields, green turnip fields, and most striking of all, were the moorelands covered with gleaming purple heather. Hawthorne hedges divided the small farm, and grew along the roadsides."

David lived in the three-room cottage with his parents, William McKay, a contractor, and his mama, Helen Oman, daughter of David Oman who managed the estate of the Earl of Caithness at Thurso, and with his siblings, Isabella, Williamena, Katherine, and Isaac.

Not only was the cottage David lived in full of beauty, but there were also other places that soothed his soul. He reminisced how he strolled down the main street, which had no particular splendor until one passed through a high, arched wall to find a magical world that appeased one's eyes on the other side. He would take in "the shining white sand, the waves rolling in with their white caps, and the Victoria Walk leading around east to the Port of Thurso, which is the safest and most sheltered port of the north for all kinds of shipping."[2]

In 1850 a thirty-seven-year-old missionary, Elder William McKay, not a relative, knocked on the McKay's door to preach the gospel to David's family. This was the same year my family became Latter-day Saints. "It took Papa several visits," David said with a gaze of remembering. "He was baptized on November third. Mama was a wee slower and waited two more days before she made the commitment to follow Papa's lead along with three of the children. They were the first converts to join in the North Country. Papa taught so much to the neighbors that he earned the name, 'The Black Minister.'"

"Black?" I asked.

David nodded. "Our clan was known as 'black' or dark-haired McKay's to tell us apart from the 'light' blond-haired clan. Papa was set apart as an elder in 1852 and became the branch president as your papa was."

"Why did your family leave?" I asked.

"My mama's family was unhappy about the new doctrine that their daughter had accepted. Other persecutions happened, and my parents felt strong impressions to come to Zion. It took a while to prepare to leave, and when all was ready, my grandparents rushed to our home to convince my mama to give up 'this mad adventure.' The pressure placed on Mama to give up this new religion was intense. 'The Presbyterian minister visited her, at the request of her family, and spent many hours arguing against her leaving.' He left her home saying, 'I am sorry to lose such a strong Christian member.' The Earl and Countess of Caithness added their pleas for her to remain, but [she] knew she was right, and nothing could change her conviction.'³

"Once all our property was sold and every arrangement made to leave, the children, including myself, became ill with the measles," David said. He cleared his throat before continuing. "My family had to wait for each of us wee ones to recover. During this time, a family friend asked my papa to borrow money, promising to pay it back when we arrived in New York. We finally left Liverpool on Sunday, May 4, 1856 on the vessel named *Thornton* and had many similar adventures as you experienced on your crossing. We traveled with 754 other saints."

"Oh, David, do not tell me that all your parents hard-earned money was stolen by that family friend?" I asked, twisting a blade of green grass in my hand.

His face reddened in blotches before he said, "It was. We could find no sign of the man anywhere. After searching thoroughly, we held a family council and decided to split up for a few years to earn the money that was needed. My older brother traveled to New Jersey to work, Papa to Connecticut, and myself to New York."

"What about your mama and sisters?"

David smiled. "They rented an upstairs apartment with only their bed as furniture."

"How did they eat?" I asked, imagining them shrinking into skeletons.

David's whole face lit up. "My mama is a very resourceful woman. She saved all the tea the ship had given out on our voyage in accordance to the word of wisdom. Therefore she had the tea to sell until money trickled in. But on with the story, we finally earned enough money to set off in a wagon from Iowa City with a company of ten to Florence, Nebraska. There we joined Captain James Brown, on June 13, 1859, to start our thousand miles."

I gasped. "That was near the time I left."

He laughed. "See, we belong together. I can tell you are like

Mama—a noble, God-fearing woman, who has much love and kindness for others. My mama went as far as to give up her seat on the wagon for a lame woman and her daughter. Mama walked the whole way to Salt Lake. We arrived on Monday, August 29, 1859."

"That was four days after us," I said, amazed at how much my family and his had similar experiences. My eyes wandered to the sky. I watched a bird's graceful movements when David surprised me again.

"I saw you soon after we arrived in Ogden."

"You did?"

"Yes, you sat on the tongue of the wagon. My family rode into town to purchase farmland and there you were. I was fifteen at the time and you merely nine. My heart was completely captured. You wore a gingham dress and pink sunbonnet, but what mesmerized me and what I could not forget were your large brown eyes."

I was flushed by this announcement and was ready for David to escort me home. Not until a later date, did David let me know of his attentions at fifteen and his intentions later were to marry me. After months of courtship and days of him working hard to earn enough money to establish a home, he asked for my hand. My parents did not like the idea. They thought I was too young and wanted me to wait until I was eighteen.

"He is a good man," I pleaded. "He follows God. He works the land and is an excellent farmer. His family is of good stock and from our part of the world. He joined the Utah militia and is under

Commander Samuel Glascow."

This last fact was both a plus and a minus for my parents. They realized that David seemed to be a social person who had a strong desire to give back to the community where he lived. On the other hand, they believed David was too young to be in the army. They laughed when they heard about what happened when David volunteered to participate in the Utah militia. Commander Samuel Glascow scrutinized my suitor with a close eye and said, "Your height is all right, but there is no hair on your face."

David had reached the required age, eighteen, and for that reason was permitted to join. Soon after that he grew a moustache, giving him an even more manly appearance.

My parents worried where this involvement with the army would take him and where it would leave me. None of us knew that David would become a captain and eventually a major in the Fifth Battalion under General Chauncey W. West. David would faithfully serve in the army until it was dissolved for political reasons. This participation eventually meant that David served on active duty in the Black Hawk War.

The Black Hawk War was a result of strained relations with the Indians in the area. Despite the fact that Brigham Young often urged the Saints to live peaceably with the Indians and to treat them with kindness, conflict arose. The Indians did not like seeing the settlers come and take away their traditional grazing, hunting, and gathering areas. The Saints thought they were treating them well and made sure land was set apart for them.

In 1864 the first reservation was created for the Indians in Utah's Uintah Basin. President Brigham Young attended treaty negotiations with the Utes at Spanish Fork in hopes to keep good relations. President Young talked with the Indian Superintendent O.H. Irish. Our prophet was successful in convincing the Utes to move onto a reservation.

Four years later the United States did not recognize this negotiation, which resulted in the Indians losing even more land. By April 1865 the Utes leader, Black Hawk, who had not attended the negotiations, gathered together bands of Indians who raided our settlements in central and southern Utah, including Richfield, Circleville, Panguitch, and Kanab. The Utes stole food, cattle, and horses. I heard talk, as I was considering whether to marry David, that the Indians stole around five thousand head of cattle and killed nearly ninety settlers and militiamen.

The conflict died down in 1870 when Black Hawk traveled to a couple of settlements and asked forgiveness. He explained that the starvation that had afflicted his people drove him to his warlike actions.

With relations still up in the air, and David's proposal made, I thought this situation over carefully. I did not know the future, but I knew I loved this man and wanted to be with no one else. I continued to beg for permission until my parents allowed this dashing man and I the privilege to have our dreams met on April 9, 1867. Thus, in the spring of my seventeenth year, we wed in the Great Salt Lake Valley at the Endowment House. We were fortunate to have the distinguished President Wilford Woodruff perform the ceremony. There in the Endowment House on Temple Square, my dear David and I began a lifelong adventure together.

Motherhood is just another name for sacrifice. From the moment the wee, helpless babe is laid on the pillow beside her, Mama daily, hourly, gives of her life to her loved one. It has been aptly said that babes draw strength at first from her bosom but always from her heart. All through the years babyhood, childhood, and youth, aye, even after her girls themselves become mamas and her sons, papas, she tenderly, lovingly sacrifices for them her time, her comfort, her pleasures, her needed rest and recreation, and, if necessary, health and life itself! No language can express the power and beauty and heroism of a mama's love.[4]

Chapter 5

HUNTSVILLE, UTAH

When to the sessions of sweet silent thought
I summon up remembrance of things past,
I sigh the lack of many a thing I sought,
And with old woes new wail my dear time's waste.
Then can I drown an eye, unused to flow,
For precious friends hid in death's dateless night,
And weep afresh love's long since canceled woe,
And moan th' expense of many a vanished sight.
Then can I grieve at grievances foregone,
And heavily from woe to woe tell o'er
The sad account of fore-bemoaned moan,
Which I new pay as if not paid before.
  But if the while I think on thee, dear friend,
  All losses are restored and sorrows end.

—William Shakespeare, Sonnet 30

Huntsville, Utah

David and I settled in Huntsville, the town he had moved to when he arrived in Deseret. It is located about thirteen miles east of Ogden, in the northern valley. The town was growing, and yet we were still one of the first settlers. David and I anticipated planting our roots there, thinking that we might have a good influence on this place.

The town became the idyllic spot—quiet, calm, neighborly, with all in the community striving to serve God. Of course there were problems, but in my biased perspective, I think we were close to creating a Zion people. The priesthood leaders did a fine job organizing the community and helping it became self-sustaining. The goal was to establish an independent commonwealth. This meant "each family owned its own home with ample acreage for a good sized vegetable garden, fruit trees, and attractive shrubbery. Each lot also had its barnyard with horses, cows, pigs, sheep, chickens, and frequently ducks and turkey."[1]

David and I owned a farm on which we raised animals, piled haystacks, and grew wheat, which we hauled to the granaries. David liked my flawless skin and white complexion, so he asked me to not ruin my looks by working in the fields. I hearkened to his request. I made sure our home was always neat and orderly and cooked the hearty food.

In the early years, David and I joined together with several neighbors and combined our cows for slaughtering. We were still a small family, and neither the neighbors nor we needed much. Sometimes in this exchange we would be lucky and added lamb and veal to our food supply. David had a special liking for those meals.

One of the tasks that David and I worked on was to make sure that we had a cow for milk, butter, and cheese; chickens for eggs, and poultry; and vegetables, which I loved to grow; and wheat to grind for bread. Every fall the community butcher traveled around to the various farms to slaughter a pig. This gave every family ham, bacon, chops, and sausage to help us make it through the winter. Another important thing for me was to slice the fat from the butchered animals. I spent many hours rendering lard to make soap. When I was not making the soap, or tending to the garden, or dinner, or cleaning, I could be found dipping candles from the wasted tallows.

The people who joined us in this tranquil land came from several different countries, and yet we were alike, united in faith. We enjoyed the various talents that came with the new people. By the time we completed our family, the town bragged many services. These "included a blacksmith shop, tin shop, a shoemaker, a wooden shoe or clog maker, two dress makers, a tailor, a milliner, a cloth weaver, a carpet weaver. A printer, butcher, basket weaver, an artificial flower maker, a flour mill, and a saw mill. In addition there was a caterer who served wedding suppers and a man who had a special formula for smoking and curing hams and bacon."[2]

From crossing the plains, to building our home, to working to establish our community into a thriving town, my husband often talked around the dinner table about the status of the railroad project the United States finally started back in 1863.

"Why are they starting the tracks in Omaha, of all places?"

I would peer at him as I placed the stew on the table. This was our routine. He rambled on in a questioning fashion about the progression of this adventure and I listened to the rhythm of his speech.

The discussion grew more tense the closer the railroad approached, and I became more interested as the railroad tracks made their way across Wyoming. Endless speculation of what would happen trickled through our town. Would Union Pacific want to include us? More than likely. How would Brigham Young lead us? Would it bring more persecution? Would this spur on another Johnston's Army incident?

The speculation began to diminish in 1868 when Union Pacific contacted Brigham Young, wanting to recruit additional labor. The negotiations began.

"Think of the opportunities the railroad could bring. It could be God's answers to how we can more effectively bring the Saints to Zion," David said.

Brigham Young saw the possibilities in a similar light. He

arranged to contribute four thousand workers to the railroad with the understanding that Mormons could immigrate to Utah at a reduced price. Plus he insisted he have a seat on Union Pacific's board of directors for himself.

Some of the workers included Brigham Young's sons Joseph A. Young, Brigham Young Jr., and John W. Young. Brigham Young's personal attorney and good friend also worked on the tracks.

On a chilly spring morning of March 8, 1869, a gentle wind danced around the Saints as we gathered in the midst of the roaring crowd. The railroad had rolled into our community, changing our isolated lifestyle forever.

David and I traveled to Ogden to celebrate the transcontinental railroad ceremony. As I listened to the cheers, watched the smiles, and listened to the laughter, I wondered what destiny the railroad had rolled in our path.

Over the years the railroad carried in immigrants, furniture, and much commercialism. This changed the Ogden community from a small farm town into the second biggest town in Utah. Three hundred immigrants from Wales, some of whom included friends of our family, were the first to chug into Ogden Sunday evening June 27, 1869. This was a glorious miracle to the building up of Zion.

I was very blessed to live such a fruitful life. Not long after David and I were married, my dear, precious Margaret Elizabeth MacKay was born. She burst into life during a snowstorm. Her earliest wails mixed with the howl of the wind as it blew against our home. The weather did not bother me because my dream of having my own child had come true. I could not believe the beautiful, pink-fleshed girl was my own. She seemed to carry the glory of an angel about her. I could not sleep after she came. Instead, I rocked by the fireplace long after Margaret slept, gazing into her perfect face. God must have surely loved me to grant the opportunity to be a mama of one such as this.

As I rocked, the overwhelming responsibility for rearing this precious child in his glory settled on me. This was the beginning of my worries as I thought often about how to clothe and feed the children. Another fear that increased as I held my child in my arms was the worry about the Indians who liked to visit. Our prophet counseled us to "feed them rather than fight with them," which is what I did when they came.

The Indians where we lived were the Shoshone and the Ute. They moved about a lot, so I never really knew when to expect them. When I was six years old, back in Iowa, I heard many gruesome tales of Indians scalping the men and stealing the women as slaves. This started a lifelong problem with nightmares of being swooped up out of David's arms into the arms of an Indian who whooped and hollered as he galloped back with me to his tribe.

David often counseled me to not worry.

"But they do mean things."

"Only when they are provoked. You are not doing that, Jennette. You feed them and treat them with utmost kindness."

I twisted my fingers in my apron in an effort to hide my fears. "But what if they get angry about what I feed them? I am used to making biscuits, vegetables, and bread and they are used to ants and grasshoppers—huge piles of them. I heard tales of them walking up to anthills, shaking off the dirt from the bugs and throwing them in their mouth!"

David would be laughing by this point, his deep chuckles. He did not take things as seriously as I. Of course he was a man and he did not have as much to worry about. There were no Indians anywhere strong enough to swoop down and carry him off. And he did not feed the people who survived off traps and snares or prey they had caught with their sinew-backed bows.

David kissed my forehead then patted my arm. "It will be all right, my dear. You gather and prepare sunflower seeds, sego lily bulbs, and arrowroot leaves just as much as they do."

"That is because I am afraid to not keep on hand what I know they will eat in case they do not like what I have prepared."

"Well, if that is the case," David said, with a smile that lit up his face, "Why don't you go hunt a mountain goat and have that in supply also?"

I would snap my dish towel at his dodging legs in response to his comment. He bellowed a deep, rich laugh that filled the cabin.

Despite my husband making light of my worries over the Indians, I was not safe. Soon enough that became apparent to him. One chilly day I had busied myself in the cabin washing clothes. I planned on getting all ready to hang them up to dry and then to finish cooking the stew when a tall dark Indian crept into my cabin.

I gasped.

He straightened his shoulders and said with a thick accent, "You be my squaw!"

This I would not have. Offering a prayer to the one mightier than all of us, I grabbed a wet towel from the washtub and swung at the waiting groom. He stepped back in startled surprised. I used this opportunity to run toward the bedroom where my husband slept. I screamed, "David, help me!"

My husband bumped into the bed trying to get to my side. The noise was loud enough for the Indian to hear and become nervous. The Indian left before my husband could do any more.

After David had held me for an extended period of time, and my beating heart settled to a slightly slower pace, I tipped my head back to look straight into his eyes and said, "I told you that there was something to fear."

He chuckled, and patted my shoulder. "You are all right dear. The Lord has protected you and he will continue to do so. Do not worry."

Thinking of how much us, the women in the Church, must manage the home front on our own, with husbands in the wheat field or mission field, reminds me of something I have not yet referred to. Since Joseph Smith's time, the Church has wanted to provide a women's organization, a society whose main focus was to provide charity for those in need. Relief Society dissolved in Nauvoo in the midst of the turmoil there.

Brigham Young tried to start the women's organization up again before the Johnston's Army marched through Utah, but due to all the panic that was involved in the episode, the organization dissolved again.

President Young was not going to let this concept fall away. He spoke about it again most plainly in the April conference of 1868. "Now, Bishops, you have smart women for wives, many of you. Let them organize Female Relief Societies in the various wards. We have many talented women among us. . . . You will find that the sisters will be the mainspring of the movement."[3]

The prophet had already set up Eliza R. Snow to be the leader. Not long after the announcement, the system was in place in our hometown. I spent many hours with the sisters, serving and working to be a blessing to others. This program turned out to be a good service. I saw it bless many lives by lifting those who were weighed down in suffering. The women's Relief Society became an integral part of the background of my life, a parallel to the brotherhood of the priesthood, sisters helping one another and the community, and learning together. Eliza R. Snow and her succeeding leaders were powerful women endowed with the gifts of the Spirit.

Returning to my life story, my family grew quickly in the first years of marriage. My second child, Ellena Odette, was my spring baby, coming on May 22, 1871. She was a delightful blonde who liked to cry through the night, keeping the entire house sleepless and exhausted. Then came an even more energetic child, David Oman McKay on September 8, 1873—our first boy. David Sr.'s eyes lit up like a flash of lightening for the first month as he carried the child around in church and on the farm, showing everyone the next David, the boy that would follow in his footsteps.

I loved seeing my husband's delight and aspirations for our son. I also had impressions of his destiny. I knew deep within my heart that this child would be an important person someday. Perhaps that knowledge made me more relaxed accepting that David O. contained so much energy that he could have supplied the railroad with enough steam to across the United States and back.

A story that shows just how much tremendous energy David O. contained when he was a toddler follows. I asked my sister, who was visiting, if she would mind watching my boy while I prepared dinner for the threshers. It was harvest time, which meant twelve hungry men lumbered in for food three times a day after working the threshing machine. The work of feeding them was daunting. My sister looked at the boy with his thick, wavy hair and plump cheeks, and thought she had the better end of the bargain.

Three hours later, as I rolled the piecrust out for dinner, my sister stormed in with David under her arm like a package, and said, face flushed, "Cooking after all the threshers would be an easier task than watching David."[4]

I took David in my arms, kissed his dirty cheek and asked, "What have you been up to?" He grabbed my lip and tugged.

"I better not say any more," my sister said. "I know all about how you snapped at our brother for teasing young David." My sister referred to the day earlier when my brother teased my son in front of a group of people. I thought he had carried his jokes too far. I told him he'd better watch himself, for my son might be an Apostle someday. He and the rest in the room gave uneasy snickers.

I switched David from one hip to the other as I continued to roll out the dough, saying to my sister. "It was nothing but the truth. David O. just might be an Apostle some day!"[5]

Other activities my husband and I became involved in, besides the farming and every day living, was to continue to help the community thrive in every way possible. We wanted to be contributing citizens who made our town a better place to live because we had been there. We got involved in the "constructing canals, irrigation ditches, building roads, bridges and public buildings. [David] gave many hours in the construction of the first school building and the first church in the valley." When a school became available for the children in the area, a problem became apparent. Many families were unable to afford the tuition.

My husband knew the importance of education and did not want to see any child needlessly miss out on the opportunity to learn. Therefore he worked with Angus McKay and William G. Smith to come up with a proposal where taxation would take the place of the tuition for each child. "The plan was adopted by all families of the community. Consequently Ogden Valley has the distinction of possessing the first free public school in the West."[6]

The United States government continued trying to creep into our lands and wanting to tell us how we were to live our lives, which kept Brother Brigham busy trying to preserve the sense that God ruled in our midst. He was also busy organizing the many different communities in what was now called Utah. We had to give up the name of Deseret because outsiders held the name to be repulsive. The name was changed to Utah, which many of the people here thought meant a "dirty, insect-infested grasshopper-eating tribe of Indians."[7]

To me, it did not matter what we called this paradise we lived in, as long as we could go on teaching our children about God and continue to worship as we wished. During all this, Brother Brigham was inspired to create a program for the children called The Primary Association.

This program did not reach us until October 20, 1880. I was thrilled to learn of this organization and even more delighted when I found out that all three of my children would be attending meetings under our first president, Moiselle Hammond Halls. She was a capable lady, well kempt, and extremely organized. To me, the best attribute that Moiselle possessed was her dedication. This was tested one afternoon when a terrible rainstorm hit Huntsville and poured water down for hours, raising the water levels to the tops of the hitching posts. The situation was extremely dangerous, but it did not hinder my children's dear teacher from swimming across a river to teach.[8]

Children continued to come into our family in what seemed to be an endless stream. I considered it a blessing. After David, there was another strong and healthy boy, Thomas Evans, who arrived during the first chill on October 29, 1875. My boys must have worn me out, for it took several years before Jennette Isabel McKay arrived on November 12, 1879. There had been a snowstorm before she was born, but that did not change the warmth I felt when I took her in my arms. She was a darling wee girl who, like the rest of my children, was blessed with thick curly hair.

David, by this time, had built a bigger home to hold all our children and the family members who liked to visit. Our extended family was in our home so often, it felt like they lived with us.

David blessed me with a twelve-room house. When we first moved in it felt luxurious, but soon all of us grew accustomed to filling the space. In our yard, the children kept busy keeping up the rhubarb patch, fruit trees, towering poplars, a barn, and the old tithing yard. David and the boys had worked hard putting up a high board fence that went around a half block.[9]

Our children worked continuously on the farm. The boys often joined their papa, who would let them choose what chore they wanted to do first. All of our children made pets out of the farm animals—horses, dogs, rabbits, so forth—and formed close attachments to them.

Sometimes owning all these animals caused a lot of commotion. One of those times I remember quite well, was when a neighbor stood with me on the front porch visiting when we noticed a stray cow in our pasture.

I called to my son who was in sight, "David, drive the animal from the field."

In response, David ran to the pasture, leaped onto his horse without a saddle or bridle, and chased the cow away. Then the young man galloped up to the front porch, coming precariously close to the visitor, and announced the job completed. He then galloped back to the pasture, jumped off his horse and turned him loose.

Once the good sister caught her breath, she turned to me and said, "Mark my words, that boy will come to no good end!"[10]

I held my tongue in fear of what would escape. I knew what this good woman said was not the truth. I would see to it that David learned the proper way to behave. I took a switch to my boy in hopes to teach him a lesson. Later I realized that was not the right way to handle him and did not do such things to my other children.

In the management of her household she was frugal yet surprisingly generous, as was papa also, in providing for the welfare and education of her children. To make home the most pleasant place in the world for her husband and children was her constant aim, which she achieved naturally and supremely. Though unselfishly devoted to her family, she tactfully taught each one to reciprocate in little acts of service.[11]

Chapter 6

O Savior, Stay This Night With Me

Abide with me; 'tis eventide.
The day is past and gone;
The shadows of the evening fall;
The night is coming on.
Within my heart a welcome guest,
Within my home abide.
O Savior, stay this night with me;
Behold, 'tis eventide.
O Savior, stay this night with me;
Behold, 'tis eventide.

Abide with me; 'tis eventide,
And lone will be the night
If I cannot commune with thee
Nor find in thee my light.
The darkness of the world, I fear,
Would in my home abide.

O Savior, stay this night with me;
Behold, 'tis eventide.
O Savior, stay this night with me;
Behold, 'tis eventide.

—Lowrie M. Hofford, "Abide with Me; 'Tis Eventide"

I have always had a sense that a mama's love was one of the most powerful weapons in protecting my children. I believed my love and devotion could protect them from the most painful things in this life. If I add to my love and devotion constant prayers in their behalf, and if I do all in my power to be obedient to God's will and teach them to do the same, I will have done everything that I could for their welfare to keep them safe from a multitude of threats. This, of course, is partly true and partly not, but believing it calmed my constant fears for their welfare.

Life was not always made of worry and fears. In winters there were good times when everyone in town gathered with bobsleds and teams of spirited horses to ride over the various hills and valleys, and then retreat to a designated home to continue the party with spicy apple cider, sugar treats, and games. In February 1880 the sleighing parties were drawing to an end, and I along with my children looked forward to the coming spring when we could plant our crops and enjoy the heat of the sun.

That February I hoped not only for spring but also for another great miracle. Earlier in the fall a panic had seized the town with rumors of a diphtheria epidemic raging through the countryside. Like many times in the past, I fell to my knees and pleaded with my Maker that the avenging angels pass our home.

Right before school came into session in fall 1879, my oldest daughter, Margaret, complained about not feeling well. Soon after, her fever crept up to extremely hot temperatures. She also suffered a severe sore throat. Fear swelled in my bosom. Margaret had only been with us for ten short years. Would God take her from us?

As memories of my siblings stricken in their youth flooded my mind, I understood on a deeper level what my mama must have suffered as she watched her children overcome with illness. I stayed up many a night, wiping a cold cloth on Margaret's forehead, trying to offer her relief. I treasured each moment in case it might be her last.

Margaret was unable to attend school as she became increasingly ill. This continued throughout the bleak winter. As the wind howled, I would tighten my grip on my apron, study Margaret's flushed face and pray over her. She valiantly fought against this illness and often asked, "How much longer until I am well, Mama?"

After what seemed like centuries, my dear daughter did receive relief from the fever, only to be racked with throbbing pain in her elbows, wrists, and knees. Strange sores appeared on her trunk and upper part of her arms and legs. Her stomach hurt and she cried for me to give relief.

Aye, I wished that a mama's love could be strong enough to

conquer all, but it was not. When the doctor came, he shook his head and reported that Margaret battled the deadly rheumatic fever. "There is so little we know about this illness. Some get better and some do not. I fear I cannot say or determine which way a patient will go."

As Margaret's illness advanced, our second child fell ail. My dear blond, curly haired Elena, nine years old, suffered an acute pain in the side of her chest, which caused her difficulty in breathing. Her coughs shook her whole frame and stole all her air. When a fit of coughing seized her, everyone stopped to listen for her breath to return. At first Elena's hacking sounded dry, but over time she produced smelly phlegm. It was strange for me to see such an active child lie lifeless in bed. She lost her appetite and developed a high fever like her sister. The doctor diagnosed her with another alarming ailment—pneumonia.

Two dreadful diseases hovered in the house. This caused fear to swell so tight in my chest that there were times I could scarcely breathe. I felt divided in my loyalties. My younger children needed to stay away from the sick, that much was clear. The responsibility of taking care of the healthy children and running the household fell on my next oldest child, David O. Fortunately for our family, David's zest for life proved a great asset, as he and his papa saw to it with that the farm and the younger children were looked after. David loved making tasks into games and had a natural way of drawing in our three-month-old Jeanette and five-year-old Thomas as I tended to the ill ones.

I spent my days and nights nursing my oldest daughters, trying to the best of my ability to will each of them back to health. They were my first children. They had taught me about the depth of emotion that is possible to feel for a child. They taught me how to be a mama. "Please, God, spare my children," I cried mightily from my heart to my Maker.

This was not to be his will. The hopes I had for the warmth of spring were mixed with fear of nursing my daughters. Margaret slipped from this life on March 28, 1880. The acute pain that I felt, then and now, I doubt I can ever adequately express. I sunk into the depths of hell where Satan attacked my soul. My faith in God and knowledge that all was not lost, and that I would see my child again, allowed me to keep putting one foot before the other. Margaret had earned her exaltation. I kept reassuring myself. She was with my siblings, with Christ, and with many loved ones. She was in the best of hands. This too kept me going.

As if burying my sweet Margaret on April 1, 1880, was not grief enough that day, dear Elena also succumbed and joined her sister in the mansions above. Knowing that the two girls were the best of friends in this world, I did not want them to be apart in the next. We buried them in the same grave to look after each other until it would be my time to join them when I could again give them my protecting eye.

On that fateful day, I went to my window boxes where I always grew flowers and had on more than one occasion donated a bouquet in celebration of the life of a lost one. I gathered all of my carnations and most of the other common garden flowers and rested them gently atop the mound that covered my children. Then I hugged the ground, hoping somehow my spirit would touch theirs. I stayed like this until David found me. He wrapped me tight in his shaking embrace. "They are in God's hands now," he whispered before my kissing my brow.

My neighbors were almost as grief stricken as we. They did every imaginable thing to help during our time of sorrow. Many women dedicated their best flowers, brought food, lent a listening ear, and offered a shoulder to cry on. I must say that we were truly blessed to live in a Zion community where such charity was shown. My family and neighbors joined together in one cause—to build up Zion. This joint mission, to live as our Savior would have us live, and trying our best, brought a confidence that could have come in no other way.

I held onto this knowledge and forged ahead, not knowing what experiences still awaited me.

Children accept mother's and father's attention, care, and devotion as they accept the pure air and the glorious sunshine—just as a matter of course—as something which is their due in this workaday world.

Until "Where is Mother?" receives no sweet response do the childish minds realize how much Mother has been to them! Not until her smile and loving presence are but sacred memories do the children know that Mother held a place in their hearts that no one else can fill! It's an unfortunate phase of human nature that it is always inclined to undervalue its present blessings, that of Mother's and Father's presence being no exception.[1]

Chapter 7

SACRIFICE

O My Luve's like a red, red rose
*   That's newly sprung in June;*
O My Luve's like the melodie
*   That's sweetly play'd in tune!*

As fair art thou, my bonnie lass,
*   So deep in luve am I;*
And I will luve thee still, my dear,
*   Till a' the seas gang dry:*

Till a' the seas gang dry, my dear,
*   And the rocks melt wi' the sun;*
I will luve thee still, my dear,
*   While the sands o' life shall run.*

And fare thee weel, my only Luve,
*   And fare thee weel awhile!*

And I will come again, my Luve,
Tho' it ware ten thousand mile.

—Robert Burns, "A Red, Red Rose"

The Calling

If it was not for the comforting arms of my husband and the peace that comes from the Spirit when I sought God's comfort, I know not how I could have made it through those next bitter months without my bonny daughters. I wandered through the mountains and canyons gazing at new life forming, reminding me of resurrection day when our sweet reunion would take place.

I was graced a year of mourning and blessed with another pregnancy before the letter arrived. The return address was The Church of Jesus Christ of Latter-day Saints, Box B. I gasped as I stared at the envelope, suspecting what it meant.

By the time boys trickled in that evening for supper, I was ready for the news that would be found in the letter waiting for David. I had prepared my husband's favorite meal—roast beef, baked potatoes, and apple pie—to ease us all into the unexpected announcement.

When David saw the letter, which I had set on his plate, his face darkened. His brow wrinkled and he looked as though a whole world of worry rested in that one letter. The children continued with their chattering, not noticing that silence had befallen their papa.

After what seemed an endless amount of time, my beloved husband cleared his throat and said, "I cannot leave you now. Not in your condition."

"Read the letter," I said.

He sighed then opened it. "It is what we feared," he said. "They want me to go back to Scotland on a mission."

I knew that my husband needed time to sort out what he wanted to do. I did not press him for answers or discussion on the matter. For two days he could not sleep or eat. I worried about him, when finally he approached me. He again cleared his throat and said, "Of course it is impossible for me to leave you and the family now. I 'decided that [I] would ask for a postponement.'"[1]

I told him without hesitation, "Of course you must accept; you need not worry about me. David O. and I will manage things nicely."[2]

"Jennette, I cannot leave you with the heavy responsibilities of running the farm and the coming of a new child."

"God will provide," was my answer. I stood from the table and gathered the dirty dishes. I would hear no more.

As I left the room, I heard my brother-in-law, John Grow, lean over to my husband and say, "You may be right, and you may be wrong; but if Jennette has set her mind that you should answer the mission call, you might as well give in! I'll keep an eye on things and help out when I can!"[3]

I could not keep a smile from bursting across my face. John had spoken well and the truth. This did not settle it with David. We continued to discuss, and in fact argue, over the matter. It was one of the only disagreements that I can remember having with my husband. I could appreciate my husband's concern. Running of the farm was a huge task to ask of anyone, especially someone in my condition, but I had my son David, who was soon to be eight and could be of assistance.

"He is too young," David Sr. would say.

"He has a lot of energy and will learn to direct it. My dear, has the thought crossed your mind that perhaps this added responsibility might be good for him? The Lord has his hand in this, and he will see to it that everything will turn out for our welfare. We owe a heavy debt to the missionaries who left their home to come and knock on our parents' doors. We need to pay back and offer the same opportunity to others who are as hungry for the truth as our parents were."

My husband would pull me on top of his lap in the rocking chair, even though I was large with child. He laughed and kissed my cheek. "You are a saint of a woman. I have that much to say of you, and it's almost completely impossible to argue with you."

After I was done smiling from his tender affections, a sly smile crept onto his face. "I guess this means that I get to ride the railroad."

I laughed. There had been many references from him about riding the rails since it first came to town at the beginning of our marriage. We could not justify paying to ride on it when the farm needed so much attention, but that did not stop David from making up excuses every several weeks for why he needed to ride it.

Later he wrote President John Taylor: "Yours of the 25th . . . I received and as you wish to know my feelings concerning the call mentioned therein, I have this to say (in short) that with the help of the Lord I will try to respond to the Call. Your Brother in the Gospel."[4]

It was much easier to be brave about doing God's will while my husband was still in the house, but once he left on April 19, 1881, I was surprised at the emptiness around us. True, there still existed the loud, fussy noise of busy children, but the place seemed like the heart was taken out of it. The first days after his departure, I played over in my thoughts his last words to our oldest son, "Take care of your Mama."[5] I had a good husband whose thoughts were on our family and my welfare above everything else but following the Lord.

Our family did not know how long David would be gone. It was normal for a missionary to be away for two to three years. When I thought of this, a heavy weight of depression spilled over me. Besides the fact that we were following the Lord's will, the only good thing I could figure in these events, was I did not need to worry that another wee one would be on its way into our home, except for the one already on its way.

It was not long, maybe hours after David left that signs started to manifest that the baby would soon arrive. This gave me renewed energy to make sure the house was in order.

I worked with David O., much the same as his papa had before he left, going over the family responsibilities with him. Though young, I will forever be grateful for his willingness to learn the jobs and to do them the best he could. I watched the pride he took in acting as the man of the house as he did the work his papa once did.

Ten days after my husband left, Ann Powell came into this world like a beautiful streak of light on April 29, 1881. She was an attractive child, full of health. I kissed her extra to make up for the two girls I lost and the kisses she would not receive until her papa returned from preaching the gospel in his homeland.

The other children took to Ann well, each loving and sometimes giving the newborn too much love. I wrote to David about her arrival. I also wrote, "Everything at home is going smoothly and we are all well, and you must not worry about us."[6] I did not tell David of any of the troubles that we had at home. I did not want his focus on us instead of doing the Lord's errand.

It was not only the newborn child we had to look after, but the planting needed to be done. David, the thoughtful man that he was, saw to it that the priesthood quorum would come over and plant. This they did. We were much appreciative. I made sure in my letters to my husband to include how well the neighbors and the Church looked after us.

David O. and his younger brother, Thomas, tended mostly to the growing of the crops and to the animals. Many times we worked side by side as the younger children played. We would talk about the scriptures, prophets, and concepts of God. It was during these occasions I was able to bear my testimony to my two sons. I hoped my words would seep into their hearts and give them the knowledge that God would always be there for them.

Although we were doing God's work, it did not mean we were spared from challenges. Many daunting tasks spread on endlessly before me. At times I felt helpless, and wished that the good Lord had granted me a man's strength. I never wrote my husband about the challenges and prayed earnestly in family prayers, morning and night, and on my own for the Lord's assistance. I knew that we could not make it on our own.

Some of the troubles we faced began right after David left. My husband, who worried about how all the hard labor would get done, arranged for a man to take care of the cattle and other heavy outside work. When this worker arrived, he brought with him a yoke of oxen, which only became an additional barnyard worry. He had not been there long when he left to visit family, leaving the oxen for young David to attend.

These oxen became an increasingly bigger burden to us. The beasts cost us dearly to feed, taking all our hard-earned hay. One day this weighed so heavily on David and me that as we dragged the hay out for the oxen to eat David hefted the hay to the animals and then turned to me with tears in his eyes and said, "Now, let's give them two large armfuls of hay and run to the house before they eat it."[7]

 ⁂

That September David O. turned eight years old. There had been talk that David O. would wait until his papa returned to be baptized. However, we were not going to put off participating in the ordinances of the gospel until it was convenient for us. Besides, I needed a man around the house who had the Spirit with him. David asked Brother Peter Gierdson to perform the baptism. Bishop Hammond of Huntsville Ward did the confirmation.

That fall I did another thing that caused people to talk. I sent my children who were old enough to school. Good-intentioned neighbors argued that I needed the children at home to help me, but I would have none of it. My children would not be deprived of their education because their papa was on a mission. I knew that my husband had similar strong feelings about the children's learning. Although he didn't want me to suffer, he would be happy that his children were securing future blessings.

If you ask me where I first received my unwavering faith in the existence of a God, I would answer you: in the home of my childhood—when Papa and Mama invariably called their children around them in the morning and at night and invoked God's blessing upon the household and upon mankind. There was a sincerity in that good patriarch's voice that left an undying impression in the souls of his children, and Mama's prayers were equally impressive.[8]

Part 2

Chapter 8

THE LADY OF SHALOTT

There she weaves by night and day
A magic web with colors gay.
She has heard a whisper say,
A curse is on her if she stay
    To look down to Camelot.
She knows not what the curse may be,
And so she weaveth steadily,
And little other care hath she,
    The Lady of Shalott.

And moving thro' a mirror clear
That hangs before her all the year,
Shadows of the world appear.
There she sees the highway near
    Winding down to Camelot;
There the river eddy whirls,
And there the surly village-churls,

And the red cloaks of market girls,
Pass onward from Shalott . . .

But in her web she still delights
To weave the mirror's magic sights,
For often thro' the silent nights
A funeral, with plumes and lights
    And music, went to Camelot;
Or when the moon was overhead,
Came two young lovers lately wed:
"I am half sick of shadows," said
    The Lady of Shalott

—Alfred, Lord Tennyson, *The Lady of Shalott* (1842)

Fear

There is something soothing about having a man in the house or out in the fields. I did not notice this until the protection was gone. Then I suddenly worried that my children and I were vulnerable.

When David was away on his mission, my fear of evil creeping onto my children and myself was almost constant. The fact that an Indian had tried to make me his bride did not help the situation. That scene replayed in my mind as proof that at any time a man could wander into our house and change our lives forever. What would have happened that day if David had not been in the other room? I dare not think about the possibilities, but I cannot avoid the contemplation.

It was well known that my husband was away to the British Isles and I was left on the farm to run it alone with my very young children. As a result, I made it a ritual to check under the beds to ensure that nothing hid waiting to attack while we slept.

I was not the only one in the house with fear of the Indians and other dangers that lurked out of our sight. Unfortunately, young David was afflicted with many of the same fears. Maybe, because we had grown so close during my husband's absence, he absorbed my fears. Perhaps our frequent Indian visitors triggered the uneasiness. I do not know.

There were several times when I was awoken at night to a trembling boy standing above my bed. "Mama, Mama."

Still in a daze, I'd mutter, "What?"

Not long after that I would be stroking his hair as he told me a dream that haunted him. "There were two giant Indians that appeared on the edge of our property. A darkness surrounded them." He shuddered.

I rested my hand on his chest to settle him.

He continued, "I ran as fast as I could go for 'The Old House,' but then a sharp pain dug into my back. As I struggled for air, I realized an arrow had hit me. I tried to get up and warn you of the danger," he said, his big earnest eyes looked in mine.

"But I couldn't move. Indians walked over me on their way to the house." His eyes teared. "Mama, is this a bad omen?"

If it were not for David and my prayers, we would have died of fright. As I wrestled with my fears, I came to know that God would protect us and that there would be an extra protection put around my family because my husband was about the Lord's work. I reminded myself to have faith when doubt bubbled up. David O. and I made a habit of constantly calling down the powers of heaven to watch over us and the other children and our farm.[1]

The Plan

After the older children left for the day, and as I busied myself with the multitude of chores, my mind worked on a scheme. At first it was a brief flash of the idea that it would be nice to involve myself in a project while David was away. I reasoned to myself that working would help make time away from my love go faster.

Right before David Sr. was called on his mission, we had paid off the last of our debts for the farm. We wanted an addition to our house, which we had often talked about doing. One day as I bathed Ann, I thought about how I could make our dream a reality. If I could earn a good profit on the harvest, then there might be enough money to hire someone to build the add-on.

I kept my idea to myself, not wanting to raise the children's hopes unless I knew I would succeed in accomplishing it. The budding plan took a devastating blow when fall came and the prices of grain fell.

I discussed this with several of my good neighbors. I heard advice that I thought held a lot of wisdom. If I held onto my crop and did not sell until spring then more than likely the price of grain would rise out of demand. I would then be able to reap a good profit.

"But Mama, how are we going to eat?" Thomas asked, after I called a family council and told them what we were about to try.

"By making things do," I said.

My children did not like this idea until I reminded them that this was their Papa's idea. "Think of his face when he comes home from serving the Lord and he sees the add-on already done."

Going without the money that we would have had that winter was extremely difficult, but by being careful, we pulled through. I rode the wagon through the mud into town that spring to learn what the grain prices would be. When I returned home that night, David and Thomas greeted me at the edge of our property.

"What happened, Mama? What price did you get?" Their faces were filled with concern. If I were David Sr., I would have put on a depressed face and then when my sons believed me, laugh and say I was joking, but I could not do that. Instead I held my arms up and yelped. The boys knew this was a good sign and immediately made plans to do the same strategy next year, too.

We worked hard the coming season and were careful with our hard-earned funds. With another spring sale of our grain, we were able to gain another increase in profit. By this point, we had enough to build the addition as had been previously planned. Our family learned the value of hard work, sacrifice, and timing to obtain a greater reward. What began as faith and was put to the test, became experience. I was so glad my children and I could obtain these things together.

Next item on the list was to find builders. "The Old House" we were living in had been built by William Christy and the missionary who had converted David's family, William McKay. Both of these brethren had moved from the Huntsville area. Therefore I spent time traveling into town and asking around for good, honest, reliable workers. I found them without once mentioning a word of the project in my letters to David.

Not only was I able to build the add-on, but I also installed a staircase. I was even more excited about the stairs than the children, if possible. Before the addition there had been "many a winter night . . . [I] had dressed warmly, gone outside, and climbed a ladder up the side of the house into the second story to tuck [my] children in bed and have evening prayers."[2] After going back outside, I would look at the evening stars and wonder what David was doing across the world. Now the interior stairs were installed and I continued to go on the porch after tucking the children in. I imagine the astonishment in David's face when he learned about what his family had accomplished with the Lord's help in his absence. I doubt he thought I had it in me.

Among my most precious soul treasures, is the memory of mama's prayers by the bedside, of her affectionate touch as she tucked the bedclothes around my brother and me and gave each a loving, goodnight kiss. We were too young and roguish, then, fully to appreciate such devotion, but we were not too young to know that mama loved us.[3]

Chapter 9

REUNION, AND MORE SACRIFICE

The expense of spirit in a waste of shame
Is lust in action, and till action, lust
Is perjured, murderous, bloody, full of blame,
Savage, extreme, rude, cruel, not to trust,
Enjoyed no sooner but despisèd straight,
Past reason hunted, and no sooner had,
Past reason hated, as a swallowed bait,
On purpose laid to make the taker mad.
Mad in pursuit, and in possession so;
Had, having, and in quest to have, extreme;
A bliss in proof, and proved, a very woe.
Before, a joy proposed, behind, a dream.
  All this the world well knows, yet none knows well
  To shun the Heaven that leads men to this Hell.

—William Shakespeare, Sonnet 129

I knew well the horrors of persecution. My mind would not let go of some of the most frightful scenes that I lived through in Wales when our family suffered religious intolerance. It seemed since David was gone, the veil of shadows that hid the most terrible events had lifted. These memories came out in my sleep, taunting me, frightening me, causing fear for my husband's safety. Many things could go wrong as he traveled across the United States to New York to board the ship, across the seas and back to Scotland. I remembered the woeful stories that both David and his parents told of the people's reactions to them joining the Church, which froze my very center. I knew well that the great adversary would go to any length to stop the building up of Zion. I also knew that God was stronger. But this did not settle my nerves as I lay down to sleep at night.

It had been so long since I had pressed my head against my husband's strong chest and listened to his heartbeat, and known that he would protect and take care of me. I did not show anyone else my doubts, my fears. I refused to allow them to get in the way of raising my children and refused to write David about them. He was not to worry about anything but doing the Lord's work. That was the safest protection for us both. I hoped he would soon return to us alive, safe, and healthy.

The time grew close when I had taken up the habit of standing atop of a rolling hill to look out over the land into the sunrise in search of the silhouette of the man I loved. I imagined many times seeing him approaching but knew it could not possibly happen that way. Truthfully, I did not care how the scene unfolded as long as he returned to me. I wanted to stare into his dark eyes, glimpsing his soul, and see his condition for myself. I would stop worrying about him when he was safely home.

After a little more than two years, in April 1883, my husband returned to us. I did not see him coming, but the children did. From my two girls' screams, I hurried from the barn to find my husband. For a long glorious moment we stared at each other in disbelief before he said, "Jennette, at last." We embraced for what seemed like hours, more real and yet more like a dream than any I had dreamed.

It took weeks for me to grow accustomed to the fact that he was back on the farm with me. He would laugh as I would reach over and touch him during the night or sometimes tap his side as I passed him in the day. I wanted the reassurance that he was there. What a blessing to have my husband return to me. The children were shy and quiet at first, but it did not take them long to warm up to David's charm and tender ways.

I had thought that we would go through an awkward stage getting reacquainted with each other. I had changed a lot being the sole provider for the farm these past years. David Sr. too had changed learning to unashamedly declare the gospel message. We did not have problems, though. When we were back together, and it felt natural, as it had always been, as though no time had passed. Something else that might have made it easier was that David was often gone with the government politics he enjoyed, and with his Church involvement he was not home enough to comment on the way I ran things.

The Lord is determined not to leave righteous men alone. There are so few of them that he must keep them busy building up Zion. Of course I do not wish for the good men to have so much required of them. Although I will make any sacrifice needed of me for this noble cause, I will admit there are those moments when I wished I could be like other women and have my husband stand by my side more often. When I thought how nice more time with my husband would be, I decided to look carefully into the character of these men that were home with their wife and don't have the constant demands from the Church. What I saw led me to count myself as blessed. There were things much worse than to have a husband that I love and adore and who loves and adores me. Things worse than to have a husband who treated me better than any queen had ever been honored. I was blessed even if I could not have him with me as much as I desired.

At times I had a feeling of gratitude swell in my heart. My husband was an honored man of God and willing to do all in his power to serve him. David Sr.'s great dedication to God influenced my children and they will follow in their papa's footsteps.

Considering how blessed I am from the merits of my husband,

it should have come to me as no surprise when, after a few weeks of being home, David was called to be the bishop in a nearby town, Eden Ward, on November 20, 1883. We accepted the position. Sunday, David would rise early and the boys, longing and needing to be with their papa, rose with him, helping him take care of the farm duties. One of the boys would ride the horse with David to town and back. David would either find a ride back that evening or walk home.

While David was gone, I would take the children to our services. The old church tower bell would ring at nine-thirty, letting everyone know that we had half an hour to get ready for Sunday School. The bell was rung again a couple minutes before ten to signal to everyone to be seated, opening exercises would begin at ten.[1]

To have my two sons David and Thomas exposed to the realities of what it was like for women who did not have a man around to carry the heavy loads was a good lesson for them. They showed a deep sensitivity to others as an outgrowth of their papa being away. They volunteered quickly to chop wood for the Church and for widows, and did many service projects.

Our situation became easier for us when David was released as bishop of the visiting town. The relief from duty was only temporary, because soon David was called to be the bishop of Huntsville Ward to replace Bishop Francis A. Hammond in March 1885.

Although David would be doing much church work, he would not need to travel as far and would have more time at home. David used the extra time to teach the boys how to be men, serve and honor God, and support oneself in farm life. Our daughters would occasionally visit and help David out in the fields, but the boys could always be found there.

Sometimes as Mamas we wonder about our children and what is going to become of them. Where will they go in their life? What is to become of them? Are we teaching them enough, guiding them, and supplying the tools necessary to properly fulfill their mission in life and be of service to the Lord? I have often pondered over the future of our children. Each one seems blessed and has a great purpose.

There are times I have been offered a glimpse of what may become of our children. The insights do not happen often and not with all of them. Many of these occasions I have regretfully forgotten, but there are a few that remain, probably because of their nature. I have thought about this particular incident many times.

My memory takes me back to the hot summer day, the sun pressing down on the farm, as I worked in the kitchen. When chores and school were completed, the boys often engaged in games of marbles and baseball. On this particular day it was marbles in the front yard. A visitor knocked on our door. Many Church leaders would stay at our home because there were no hotels or restaurants in the town. I learned to be prepared for this great honor. It happened so often I left my full-length table out in the dinning room and did up the guest room.

Patriarch John Smith stood at our front door. He did much traveling for the Church, making his rounds, giving patriarchal blessings to the local members in the nearby three wards. He would often stay at our house for several weeks at a time.

This day Brother Smith decided to give my oldest living child, David O. a blessing. In the blessing he said:

> Brother David Oman McKay, thou art in thy youth and need instruction, therefore I say unto thee, be taught of thy parents the way of life and salvation, that at an early day you may be prepared for a responsible position, for the eye of the Lord is upon thee . . . The Lord has a work for thee to do, in which thou shalt see much of the world, assist in gathering scattered Israel and also labor in the ministry. It shall be thy lot to sit in council with thy brethren and preside among the people and exhort the Saints to faithfulness.[2]

To know that our children were on course to serve God was a mighty knowledge and one that I could not take lightly. I increased my efforts in raising our children, not only with David but also with the others. If God wanted them instructed well so they could serve others, then I would see to it that I did my part.

As Brother Smith left, he passed David on the way out of the house, put his hand on my boy's shoulders and said, "My boy, you have something to do besides playing with marbles."[3]

We watched Brother Smith climb on his horse and ride away. I returned to the kitchen to finish preparing dinner. David followed me. I looked at David O., sensing that he was upset. He wrinkled his brow in a serious fashion and said, "If he thinks I'm going to stop playing marbles, he is mistaken."[4]

Knowing that this was very important to David, I said an earnest prayer in my heart that I would be guided to the right things to say. Then I sat at the kitchen table and discussed with him what Brother Smith meant.

The frequent visits of church leaders at times became exhausting. Some of the authorities that visited were: the Weber Stake presidency, Lewis W. Shurtliff, Charles F. Middleton, and Nels C. Flygare. They became close family friends from visiting so often. The stake officers of the auxiliary organizations were common visitors as well. Some of those individuals were: Jane S. Richards, Emily Shurtliff, Harriet Brown, Josephine West, Elizabeth Standford, Aunt Rose Canfield, my wonderful former teacher, and Harriet Woodmansee. When thoughts came to mind about how nice it would be to have our house to ourselves, I would say, "They always leave a blessing in our home, so we are happy to have them."[5]

An example of the great blessings our visitors bestowed can be seen in this simple story. The year was 1889, and it was time for my dear Ann to get baptized along with three of her cousins. The extended family had gathered at the nearby swimming hole. This event I am ashamed to say had become commonplace in our attitude. We were complacent to the sacredness of this ordinance.

On our way back from the pool we came upon Elder Richard Ballantyne, George Goddard, and William Willis of the Church Sunday School. They had come to stay at our home to attend the conference the next day. Ann invited them to attend her and her cousins' confirmation.

They accepted with pleased smiles. Later that night the men joined in the family prayer. Elder Goddard was asked to say it. He graciously accepted. He poured his heart out in gratitude for the privilege of witnessing the young peoples becoming members of the Church earlier that day.

The sacred nature of this prayer had a profound effect on my children. I could see it in their faces after they said amen. I could also hear it in their speech. They realized they had taken the Church ordinance lightly but have never done so since.

Not only were my children's testimonies strengthened from being in the presence of the men in leadership, but they were exposed to great minds and literature. Elder Orson F. Whitney of the Council of the Twelve liked to stay in our home and sit by the fireplace composing his poems, which he would read to our family.

We enjoyed hearing the artist at work and appreciated his gift of spinning words. We were thrilled when he sent us an auto-graphed copy of his poems. We treasured this gift. Not only did we love to read the words, but it has inspired the children to write and read great literature. He did a fine job in opening up the minds of my daughters.

To this day, many of our children have manifested great interest in literature. Some have taken much time memorizing and quoting it, which delights me much. Some have even taught about the merits and composition of the literature works to others. I believe Elder Whitney did a great job of influencing my children, while my encouragement fell on deaf ears.

Another benefit from having the frequent visitors was that my children learned self-constraint. At times there was not enough food for everyone to indulge. In order to make sure that our guests were well taken care of, I came up with the code word FHB. When my children heard me say FHB, they knew that it meant "Family Hold Back" or in other words, do not eat much of the food. Thomas and William hated the phrase and would wrinkle their noses and give me pleading eyes to change my mind. Ann would seem as though she thought it was a great blessing to sacrifice for the Lord's servants. Interesting how their responses could be so different.

An exciting time occurred when the General Relief Society President, Eliza R. Snow, stayed with us. She spoke at the conference in Huntsville, where David O. and several of his deacon friends sang in the meeting. They did a fine job, except for the few notes that came out flat and that they held back on the volume. This did not stop Sister Snow from prophesying. She said, "I can see in that group of boys bishops of wards, presidents of stakes, Apostles, and some of you will live to see the Savior."[6]

I think the visit that I will cherish the most was when the First Presidency of the Church came. This included President Wilford Woodruff and his counselors, George Q. Cannon and Joseph F. Smith. Those men brought with them such a powerful and yet comfortable presence. This spirit that they possessed radiated from them and filled the whole house, settling the children and uplifting my tired spirit.

While the men ate at the table, Ann played quietly with baby Morgan in the other room. The men noticed, and after eating President Wilford Woodruff walked in the other room, picked up the baby, and nestled him in his arms. A smile exuded from him. "What a lovely child." The prophet proceeded to give my son a blessing. What a cherished gift. I thought it that many times as I watched Morgan grow. What a privilege he had been granted. Did my son Morgan know whose presence he had been in?

Sometimes the thought that I have entertained the prophet and the First Presidency is overwhelming. I would have never imaged a girl from a remote town in Wales would be here in Utah, associating with the Lord's anointed, even the prophet himself. If I would have tried my best, I could have never come up with that event for myself or for my children. I have been blessed indeed.

From my beautiful, ever devoted, and watchful mother, from my loyal sisters in our early home associations, and from my beloved wife during the maturer years that followed, I have received my high ideals of womanhood. No man has had inspiration from nobler, more loving women. To them I owe a debt of eternal gratitude.[7]

Chapter 10

EDUCATION

The mountain and the squirrel
Had a quarrel;
And the former called the latter "Little Prig."
Bun replied,
"You are doubtless very big;
But all sorts of things and weather
Must be taken in together,
To make up a year
And a sphere.
And I think it no disgrace
To occupy my place.
If I'm not so large as you,
You are not so small as I,
And not half so spry.
I'll not deny you make
A very pretty squirrel track;
Talents differ; all is well and wisely put;

If I cannot carry forests on my back,
Neither can you crack a nut."

—Ralph Waldo Emerson, *Fable*

Education has always been important in our family. I wanted my children to gain the knowledge I did not have. My children grew tired of hearing me lecture them about the importance of learning.

"We know, Mama, we know," they would say.

David was our first to graduate from eighth grade in the local school. Since the Church also encouraged education, they asked that each stake supply an academy of learning for the next stage of education.

On August 19, 1889, we sent David O. to Weber Stake Academy, which was in its second year, along with seventy other students. He was to meet in the ward building and stay with my mama. I often encouraged all my children to learn the Welsh language, but David O. would hear none of it. I am sure while he stayed with my dear mama he regretted this decision, for Mama was older and would often slip into her native tongue. He did tell the younger children to learn it. Katherine and Morgan listened to his counsel.

I often think about my son living on Twenty-Eighth Street and Lincoln Avenue in Ogden, with my Welsh mama chattering to him in a language he did not know. In the fall, when I left him, the street was filled with the rich smell from the apple orchard and currant bushes. It truly would be a growing experience for him.

David eventually thrived at the school. He reported that many students came and left. David O. was steadfast in learning the most he could and eager to have his siblings join in the opportunities. He stayed at the academy for two years, returning later as a teacher to the school he had attended as a boy.

Meanwhile my family continued to grow. William Monroe was two years old when David first left. William was as busy as ever David was. Unlike David, he hated the feeling of dirt. When he got his clothes wet, he would want them changed.

In the winter of 1891, in February, Katherine Favourite was born. Thankfully she was a quiet child who enjoyed sleep. I did not know if I could have kept up otherwise. Having children was getting harder. I could feel my age.

Our children were in such different stages, it was an interesting period in our life. Times were both harder and easier on David Sr. and I. We missed David O. and knew that soon other of our older children would leave. Chasing after the younger children was exhausting, but we had more chasers to help us.

David Sr. saw to it that the family ran smoothly, like he had with the city work and the different offices he held with the Church administration. He laid out a system where an older child was responsible for the needs and cares of a younger child. It worked well.

When our oldest son returned from school, he very much

wanted to continue attending more. Thomas, Jeanette, and Ann were also ready for advanced schooling, but our funds could not stretch far enough to provide all our children with this opportunity. This realization sickened me, and I often resorted to prayer.

One bright, sunny morning, when all seemed lost, I stood in my yard, taking in the landscape, the sky, and listening to the birds' song when a gift arrived in the mail from my mama. Tears brimmed my eyes. I could not believe my mama's goodness and God's hand in it. Mama had sent each one of her children $2,500.

In the letter, Mama suggested that I put the money in stocks, hearing I could make a lot of profit that way. I would hear none of it. I said, "Every cent of this goes into the education of our children."[1]

This was an opportunity that very few around us were allowed. I felt blessed that the Lord had somehow provided a way for this to happen. My children were good students and would not slack in their studies.

We set up a system where David and Jeanette would go to the University, and then they would teach to keep Thomas and Ann in school. This way the money could be spread out and benefit the younger children. David and Jeanette readily agreed to it, feeling overwhelmed with gratitude that they had been blessed.

Time passed and another baby came to us on June 25, 1893. The pregnancy and birth were more draining than the others. Since Morgan Powell was born, I have not felt myself. With celebrating the birth of the tenth child coming into this world, I had a deep knowing that Morgan would be my last. I could not survive another birth. I felt a sadness, because after my beautiful bald lad was born I lacked the strength to enjoy his beginning months that I had treasured with my other children.

Despite that, visitors loved to come to our home and dote on Morgan, and like all good youngest, he soaked up as much attention as he could. Sometimes this meant that he came up with a prolonged routine of toddler tricks to entertain the guests.

In 1894, four of our children: David, Thomas, Jeanette, and Ann set out in late summer with the heat still warming the earth. They "rolled over the sand ridge from Huntsville with horse and wagon, a cow in the trailer . . . a sack of flour milled from wheat [they] had grown, [and] jars of fruit"[2] I had prepared for them. My children had launched off on a grand adventure at the University of Utah. My husband found them lodging in Union Square.

While our children attended school I missed them terribly and looked forward to when they would make trips to the farm to celebrate a holiday or the summer with us. David Sr. would not admit to missing the children, but he often said, "I wonder what David, Ann, Jeanette, or Thomas would think about this latest city hall development."

He wrote them more often than I. He penned essays on politics and Church happenings. I often smiled as David Sr. sat at his desk composing his latest correspondence. "Writing a book?" I asked.

He would laugh and give me a kiss. "Yes, my dear. Would you like me to tell them anything from you?"

When our students returned to us, they were full of stories and new ideas that they wanted to try out. Watching young minds open and grasp knowledge was fascinating. Sooner than I wanted, the summer ended and it was time for our older children to depart from us to attend school once again. This time I wanted to see where they lived and spend more time with our children before they became completely immersed in their studies.

They had made new living arrangements and rented a cottage in the back of Emma Louisa Riggs and her family's house on Second West. This was where David O. would eventually fall in love with Emma's daughter, Emma.

One never truly knows what the Lord has in store for them; neither do they know how their actions can affect others and what a small world we live in. This became ever clearer to me after hearing what happened to two little girls in distress I had helped.

The story began when I traveled to the University of Utah to visit my children. I had missed them terribly and wanted to make sure that they were being taken care of and eating right. While there, the children and I decided to attend the theater. We did so and much enjoyed the production. We were discussing various themes we thought the producers had brought out in the play, when suddenly a woman screamed in a nearby house. David O. thought that the woman was being beaten by her husband and ran to her house and banged on the window to stop the assault. My resourceful Thomas ran to the fire station to call the police.

The elderly landlady of the house arrived on the scene with a key in hand and muttered under her breath before the police arrived. When she opened the door, a woman stood with tangled hair, eyes glazed over, and what looked like an alcoholic drink in her hand. Her house smelled like a tavern and was in disarray, nothing looked tended to.

Beyond the woman, stood two wee girls whose eyes had grown red from crying. My heart reached out to those little ones who had no choice but to be subjected to such a life. I could think of nothing else to do but to bring the two into my arms and comfort them, which I did. Those girls' hearts raced and their eyes opened wide. How could a person do that to their children? What miserable lot in life would cause someone to choose this evil in the holy nation that we strove to establish? This scene reminded me of many of the sad things I had witnessed in Wales and wished did not happen.

Several years after this happened, David O. wrote to inform me that he discovered that these sweet girls had made it to reform school where he taught. They were anxiously engaged in making their lives better than where they had come from. My prayers often went out to those tender lasses and to their mama, who must have been in awful misery.

It is only an old country home, but no place was ever filled with truer love and devotion on the part of the parents, brothers, and sisters, than those which pervaded the hearts of the loved ones in that family circle. [When] I walked out of the front door, as the night latch clicked, I thought it might have been the click of the lid of a treasure chest that held the wealth of memories that no money could buy.[3]

Chapter 11

The Final Years

My Mama! God bless you!
For your purity of soul,
Your faith, your tenderness,
Your watchful care,
Your supreme patience,
Your companionship and trust
Your loyalty to the right,
Your help and inspiration to papa,
Your unselfish devotion to us children.

—David O. McKay

It has been a great honor as a mama to watch my children grow older and begin to show the first signs of blooming into the wonderful adults that they would become. I hope I can be around to witness their unfolding. My university children were fun to watch—their minds on fire with knowledge. While they were away at college, I heard a lot about their university life—the dances, their romances, teachers, tests, and the friends they made. My children had formed a friendship with Stephen L. Richards and had spent many a pleasant evening in conversation with him at his home in Salt Lake. I could think of no better way for them to spend their time.

School was of utmost importance to them. The older children were eager to earn their degrees and secure teaching jobs to supply the money needed for the younger children to have the same opportunities. The younger children missed their older brothers and sisters, but their interests were set on the latest baseball game, the upcoming church event, or the soon-to-be announced dance. Life seemed to be moving ahead in a pleasant flow when another letter arrived from the Church, addressed to David O. with the return address Box B.

David O. did not at first take kindly to the news. He had graduated from University of Utah as valedictorian with a teaching certificate and plans to teach for Salt Lake County. He much wanted to see that his other brothers and sisters had the same opportunity that he was allotted. I must admit my heart was set on that arrangement and so were the younger children's. I spent many a night talking with the younger ones about their future and God's hand in their lives.

My oldest boy did not want to go on the mission he was called to. He put up a great fuss. His papa and I had many talks with him. We reminded him that no one in our family had ever turned away a call, even though it came at inopportune times. I bore testimony of my gratitude to the missionaries who had sacrificed to journey to my home in Wales and to his papa's home in Scotland.

David O. worried about the other children. My husband reassured him that things would be fine. Believing what we told him was the truth, David O. sat down and wrote this letter to Elder George Reynolds:

> Since giving you a verbal answer about my mission, I received your communication requesting me to submit my answer in writing. I cheerfully do so by saying that I shall be ready to start a mission to Europe on the 7th of Aug.
>
> Hoping to get a prompt reply stating what country I shall be assigned to, and praying for the blessings of God to attend all those promulgating the principles of truth,
>
> I remain,
>
> Your brother in the gospel,
>
> David O. McKay[1]

His letter was longer and fancier than the one his papa had written all those years ago, but I could not help but be taken back to my husband's call when we were asked to make such a huge sacrifice. Now it was our oldest son's turn. By being willing to serve God, I felt reassured that God would bless him much, and David O. would learn many of the soul lessons that could only be learned by making such sacrifices.

Things have a way of working out and they did for our boy.

David O. was ordained to a seventy and we said our good-byes on August 1, 1897 as he headed to Great Britain. I held my tears back, but the children did not. They loved their older brother and thought it was quite a sacrifice to be asked to do without him for a few years.

Before David O. left he was given a blessing, which said that he would return to us safely. Although my heart hurt to separate from my dear boy, I trusted that he was doing God's will and all would be fine. The family and I wrote him often, especially the younger children. They enjoyed making cards for David O. to let him know that he was still in our thoughts and prayers.

I enjoyed the correspondence I had with him while he was on his mission. Even though he was almost a whole world apart, he wrote us often and sent us Christmas presents. For Christmas on 1898, I received fine gloves, and my husband was sent a handsome handkerchief. David O.'s thoughtfulness pleased us.

David did return safely, and his testimony and strength of character had blossomed. Sometimes I could not help staring at him, admiring the growth. In fact I have done this with all our children. It seemed each one was turning into a person God would be pleased with. What a rich treasure for a mama. I could ask for no better gift.

My children were growing older and moving forward in earning their education, creating families, and serving the Lord. It has been a great joy for me to see our grandchildren come to earth. I love holding them in my arms and trying to figure out what they have to teach me. These wee ones have recently left heaven and still have its glow about them.

As our grandchildren became toddlers, I wondered how I ever had the strength to keep up with them. How did I manage to run the farm? Aye, it was a mystery, but I feel confident I was blessed by God to do all that I was required as a mother and wife.

The older children are adults in their own right now, and the younger ones are soon to follow. It is with much delight I witness the close friendships and support they are forging with one another. There is much love between them and they talk often about living close to each other.

David Sr. and I have already established a strong tradition of living close to family—cousins, aunts, uncles, and grandparents. I hope that my children will continue in this lifestyle, for truly there is much happiness and support that can be felt in being so close to family. Many a summer my children played with their cousins. Their favorite pastimes were: baseball, croquet, reading, swimming, Rook, listening to the funny old stories, and sometimes the serious ones. My husband had crafted a stunning croquet course behind our house. Gooseberries grew close by. It was common during a game for the players to nibble gooseberries waiting their turn. The children also helped each other with their various duties on the farm so they could play.

A smile comes to my face as I think about the children gathering in our barn with the huge lofts of hay. My husband's signature of excellent craftsmanship showed on the barn, as well as with everything else he built. He used a sandstone foundation and beams an inch thick to ensure the strength of the structure.

Another aspect about the farm that my husband took great pleasure in was cultivating his garden. He was "so particular about the soil that he wouldn't walk on the ground between the rows when he was planting. He carefully laid out one-by-twelve planks that we all had to stay on when we came into his garden."[2] The pride of David Sr.'s garden was his huge raspberry patch and the special red rhubarb that he had brought from Scotland.

Besides the social activity, our family supported each other in many other ways. When David O. was on his mission in the British Isles, they wrote to him faithfully. Our children showed the same support to Tommy when he was called to Germany and served his mission.

Our two older boys turned out to look very much like each other. This has caused some confusion in the community. An acquaintance once commented on it when he finally saw David and Tommy together at the railroad station. He said, "Now I understand why David O. McKay sometimes greets me affably and sometimes ignores me. This [pointing to David] is the David O. McKay who always speaks to me and this [pointing to Tommy] is the David O. McKay who ignores me."[3]

God has been good to me all my days. I owe him for the blessings he has bestowed on me. I think about the greatness of God as the wind in Huntsville grows colder. The storm will be here soon. I wonder if I have yet to live more of life, or are my days becoming numbered? It is 1905 and I am fifty-three years old.

I miss my parents and my siblings that I lost long ago in Wales and more recently here in Utah. But mostly the lifelong ache continues for my two bonny, oldest daughters. Having them ripped from me when they were just beginning to live life seems so cruel, yet I really cannot complain.

I look at my neighbors and realize the same types of sorrows have beset them. My suffering was not unlike theirs and I know if I had stayed in Wales I would have lost many more of my dear children, as my mama had. Those times were hard, peppered with lots of misery. Everyone struggled there.

These trials I know make us stronger and made my faith more solid. I do not regret them. Often now I think of the glorious day when I will reunite with my daughters, taking them in my arms again. I long for the time when I have all my family with me and we kneel at Jesus' feet.

Mother left us when she was still young, only fifty-four. During the intervening twenty-seven years I have often wished that I had told her in my young manhood that my love for her and the realization of her love and of her confidence gave me power more than once during fiery youth to keep my name untarnished and my soul from clay.[4]

Afterword

Jennette Eveline Evans McKay died on January 6, 1905, of a stroke in her home. The weight of her responsibilities took much out of her and caused her health problems. She was buried in Huntsville, Utah.

The *Salt Lake Tribune* reported, "Few women in Weber County were more widely known or more universally loved than Mrs. David McKay, and the announcement of her death has caused a gloom of sorrow not only throughout Ogden City and Weber County but also over the entire state."[1]

Jennette's husband, David, was heartbroken from her passing. He felt her absence intensely. He never desired or would think about remarriage. Feeling strongly that a bishop should be married, David resigned from his calling over the Huntsville Ward. He served on in the high council and as stake patriarch. David Sr. had the privilege of having his son, David O., the Apostle, set him apart. David Sr. also continued to keep himself busy as he worked as a loyal board member of Weber Academy. He joined his dear wife in heaven twelve years after her passing, in November 1917.

The many prophesies that were given of her son began to come true a year after Jennette's death, when David O. McKay was called to the Quorum of the Twelve by President Joseph F. Smith. John W. Taylor and Matthias F. Cowley had resigned from the Quorum to enable themselves to preach and practice polygamy in Canada and Mexico, acting against the Second Manifesto, which declared polygamy was not to be practiced. A third position in the Quorum of the Twelve was left vacant when Apostle Marriner W. Merrill passed away.

David O. McKay contributed to the way the Sunday school is currently run and was actively involved in developing the Church welfare system. The prophecy of travel came to pass when, as an Apostle, he left for a one-year tour with Elder Hugh J. Cannon to visit Church missions around the world. He again fulfilled this prophecy after being sustained as the ninth President of the Church on April 9, 1951, and he embarked on a nine-week tour of Europe, making him the first traveling prophet.

David served for nineteen years and became one of the most beloved prophets. The Church membership grew from one million to three million under his term.

The love, admiration, and adoration that David O. had for his mama is strongly woven through his dissertations and addresses. He had a great love for her and sorely missed her after her passing.

Jennette and David Sr.'s son Thomas became an Assistant to the Twelve Apostles. Their daughter, Jeanette McKay Morrell, continued her studies at University of Chicago and was active and held important positions in the General Federation of Women's

Clubs. She also served on several medical and educational committees in Utah.

Jennette's influence has and will continue to affect millions as people become acquainted with her spirit through the words of appreciation and reflection of her son, the prophet David O. McKay.

In March 1961 President McKay returned to Wales to break ground in Merthyr Tydfil for a Latter-day Saint chapel and to unveil a commemorative plaque the prophet had granted permission to be placed at his mama's birthplace. The monument reads:

Birthplace of
JENNETTE EVELINE EVANS
Born in Plas-Helygen,
69 Clywdyfagwyr
Merthyr Tydfil,
Glamorganshire, South Wales
Born August 28, 1850
Died January 6, 1905
At Huntsville, Utah

United States of America
Emigrated with her family
To America May 22, 1856
Married David McKay on
April 9, 1867 in Ogden, Utah
They were parents of ten
Children, of whom their
Eldest son and third child,
DAVID OMAN MCKAY
Became the Ninth President
Of The Church of Jesus Christ
Of Latter-day Saints on
April 9, 1951

Endnotes

Chapter 1

1. In Conference Report, April 1951, 157, 159.

2. Morrell, *Highlights in the Life of President David O. McKay*, 6.

3. McKay, *Gospel Ideals*, 123.

4. Thomas Rees, in *Recollections of Merthyr's Past*, 5.

5. Rees, 6.

6. McKay, *Home Memories of President David O. McKay*, 25.

7. McKay, *Gospel Ideals*, 123.

8. Ibid., 123.

9. McKay, *Home Memories of President David O. McKay*, 1.

Chapter 2

1. McKay, *Home Memories of President David O. McKay*, 83.

2. *Millennial Star* 17 (22 December 1855).

3. McKay, *Home Memories of President David O. McKay*, 25.

4. Ibid., 1.

Chapter 3

1. From Eliza R. Snow, "Poems"; reprinted in *Millennial Star*, 22 March 1856.

2. Brigham Young, in *Journal of Discourses*, 5:232.

3. Morrell, *Highlights in the Life of President David O. McKay*, 6.

4. Ibid.

5. Angelina Calkins Farley diary, 22 September 1850, microfilm of holograph, LDS Church Archives.

6. Godfrey and Derr, *Women's Voices*, 6.

7. Young, in *Journal of Discourses*, 15:223.

8. Arrington, et al., *Mothers of the Prophets*, 148.

9. Ibid.

10. Godfrey and Derr, 8.

11. David O. McKay to Lou Jean McKay, aboard the *SS Tofua*, 5 May 1921, McKay Papers, MS 668, box 1, folder 5, Manuscripts Division, University of Utah Marriott Library, Salt Lake City; this letter is reproduced in part in McKay, *My Father, David O. McKay*, 130–32.

Chapter 4

1. Terry, *David O. McKay: Prophet of Love*, 12, 14.

2. Morrell, *Highlights in the Life of President David O. McKay*, 5.

3. Ibid.

4. McKay, *Gospel Ideals*, 447–57.

Chapter 5

1. Morrell, *Highlights in the Life of President David O. McKay*, 8.

2. Ibid.

3. Brigham Young, in *Journal of Discourses*, 12:201.

4. Ernest L. Wilkinson, "David O. McKay Building Dedication," *BYU Speeches of the Year* (Provo, Utah: Brigham Young University, 1954), 2.

5. Marie F. Felt, "David, a Boy of Promise," *The Instructor*, September 1969, 329.

6. McKay, *Home Memories of President David O. McKay*, 12.

7. Powell, *The Encyclopedia of Utah*, 84.

8. Ibid.

9. David O. McKay to Lou Jean McKay, aboard the *SS Tofua*, 5 May 1921, McKay Papers, MS 668, box 1, folder 5, Manuscripts Division, University of Utah Marriott Library, Salt Lake City; this letter is reproduced in part in McKay, *My Father, David O. McKay*, 130–32.

10. Terry, *David O. McKay: Prophet of Love*, 25.

11. McKay, *Home Memories of President David O. McKay*, 1.

Chapter 6

1. McKay, *Gospel Ideals*, 454–55.

Chapter 7

1. Thomas E. McKay, in Conference Report, April 1952, 24.

2. McKay, *Home Memories of President David O. McKay*, 3.

3. Ibid.

4. David McKay to President John Taylor, 27 March 1881, film CR1/168, reel 1, 937, LDS Church Archives.

5. Morrell, *Highlights in the Life of President David O. McKay*, 11.

6. Ibid.

7. Ibid.

8. McKay, *Teachings of Presidents of the Church—David O. McKay*, 74.

Chapter 8

1. McKay, *Gospel Ideas*, 524.

2. Madsen, *Mothers of the Prophets*, 224.

3. McKay, *Home Memories of President David O. McKay*, 1.

Chapter 9

1. Morrell, *Highlights in the Life of President David O. McKay*, 9.

2. Ibid., 12.

3. Ibid.

4. Ibid.

5. Ibid.

6. John C. Peterson to President David O. McKay, 19 December 1955, McKay Scrapbook, no. 188.

7. McKay, *Home Memories of President David O. McKay,* 4.

Chapter 10

1. Morrell, *Highlights in the Life of President David O. McKay,* 31.

2. McKay, *Home Memories of President David O. McKay,* 9.

3. Arrington, *Mothers of the Prophets,* 151–52.

Chapter 11

1. David O. McKay to Elder George Reyonds, 29 June 1897, CR 1/68, box 12, folder 18, LDS Church Archives.

2. McKay, *My Father, David O. McKay,* 68.

3. Ibid., 69.

4. McKay, *Home Memories of President David O. McKay,* 4.

Afterword

1. In McKay, *Home Memories of President David O. McKay,* 148–49.

References

Alexander, Thomas G. *Utah the Right Place (Revised and Updated Edition).* Layton, Utah: Gibb Smith, 2002.

Arrington, Leonard J. *The Presidents of the Church.* Salt Lake City: Deseret Book, 1986.

Arrington, Leonard J., Susan Arrington Madsen, and Emily Madsen Jones. *Mothers of the Prophets.* Salt Lake City: Bookcraft, 2001.

Conference Reports of The Church of Jesus Christ of Latter-day Saints. Salt Lake City: The Church of Jesus Christ of Latter-day Saints, 1898 to present.

Derr, Jill Mulvay, Janath Russell Cannon, and Maureen Ursenbach Beecher. *Women of Covenant: The Story of the Relief Society.* Salt Lake City: Deseret Book, 1992.

Garr, Arnold K., Donald Q. Cannon, and Richard O. Cowan, ed. *Encyclopedia of Latter-day Saint History.* Salt Lake City: Deseret Book, 2000.

Godfey, Kenneth W., and Jill Mulvay Derr. *Women's Voices: An Untold History of the Latter-day Saints.* Salt Lake City: Deseret Book, 1982.

Goodman, Drew S. *The Fulness of Times: A Chronological Comparison of Important Events in Church, U.S., and World History.* Salt Lake City: Eagle Gate, 2001.

Hafen, Leroy R., and Ann W. Hafen. *Handcarts to Zion: The Story of a Unique Western Migration, 1856–1860.* Spokane, Wash.: Bison Books, 1992.

Holzapfel, Richard Neitzel, and William W. Slaughter. *Prophets of the Latter Days.* Salt Lake City: Deseret Book, 2003.

Journal of Discourses. 26 vols. London: Latter-day Saints' Book Depot, 1854–86.

Kelly, Brian, and Petrea Kelly. *Latter-day History of The Church of Jesus Christ of Latter-day Saints.* American Fork, Utah: Covenant, 2000.

Larson, Stan, and Patricia Larson. *What E'er Thou Art Act Well Thy Part: The Missionary Diaries of David O. McKay.* Salt Lake City: Blue Ribbon Books, 1999.

Madsen, Susan Arrington. *Mothers of the Prophets.* Salt Lake City: Deseret Book, 2001.

McKay, David Lawrence. *My Father, David O. McKay.* Salt Lake City: Deseret Book, 1989.

McKay, David O. *Gospel Ideas: Selections from the Discourses of David O. McKay.* Salt Lake City: Improvement Era, 1953.

———. *Teachings of Presidents of the Church: David O. McKay.* Salt Lake City: The Church of Jesus Christ of Latter-day Saints, 2003.

McKay, Llewelyn R. *Home Memories of President David O. McKay.* Salt Lake City: Deseret Book, 1956.

Morrell, Jennette McKay. *Highlights in the Life of President David O. McKay.* Salt Lake City: Deseret Book, 1966.

Powell, Allan Kent, ed. *Utah History Encyclopedia.* Salt Lake City: University of Utah Press, 1994.

Recollections of Merthyr's Past. Risca, Wales: Starling Press, 1979.

Roberts, Richard C., and Richard W. Sadler. *A History of Weber County: Utah Centennial County History Series.* Weber, Utah: Utah State Historical Society, 1997.

Smith, Barbara B., and Blythe Daryn Thatcher, ed. *Heroines of Restoration.* Salt Lake City: Bookcraft, 1997.

Terry, Keith. *David O. McKay: Prophet of Love.* Santa Barbara, Calif.: Butterfly, 1980.

Woodger, Mary Jane. *David O. McKay: Beloved Prophet.* American Fork: Covenant, 2004.